HOW TO SAVE A SMALL FORTUNE – AND THE PLANET

A Practical Guide to Smart, Sustainable Spending Beyond COVID-19

R.A. DALKEY

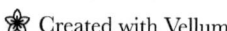

Contents

Getting Started

Introduction

That was a shock, wasn't it?

COVID-19 has shaken us up like nothing since World War II. Some people saw a phenomenon of that magnitude coming; most didn't. But we've all been hit in some way.

Maybe you lost your job or had your hours cut. Maybe you're still on the staff, but you're not sure how long that's going to last. Or perhaps you've suddenly concluded that your job isn't ethical and supports a system that doesn't deserve your participation. Perhaps you want to start doing something more meaningful and impactful — but which could involve earning less.

What to do?

Whatever your situation, now is the moment to understand that *earning less money doesn't have to be a problem.* That reducing the amount that leaves your bank account is as powerful a strategy as topping it up. That spending time on the former is as legitimate as spending time on the latter. Grasp this reality, and you can consider yourself liberated. You've now got a ton more options.

It's a simple logic. But one to which most of us are blind.

Why don't we see it? Because our world is all about 'earn more, earn more, earn more'; 'get more, get more, get more'; and 'buy more, buy more, buy more'! Earning through labour is healthy and honest, while savers are masochistic miseries. Or so we're told.

Yet the fact remains that you can reach any given status — financially speaking — by *earning less* and *saving more*. Better habits and wiser spending decisions are as good as a pay rise. But our culture doesn't want you to see that halving your expenses is no different from doubling your salary.

Unfortunately, that clouding of reality isn't likely to change much even when we finally emerge from COVID-19. Which is why it's more critical than ever to see these truths that your parents, your teachers and (if you prefer) 'the system' never shared with you.

But helping you stretch your money is just one part of what this book is about.

The other part is tied up with those uncomfortable (and more nagging than ever) ethical challenges I mentioned. I want to point out the multitude of ways in which you can contribute to a cleaner, more sustainable Earth *through the act* of saving money.

Perhaps it's no coincidence that the same colour — green — is associated with both a positive bank balance and environmentally sound behaviour. Because when you learn the good habits of saving money, you're also learning the good habits we need to fix the planet's increasingly obvious problems. It's very rare that saving money doesn't sit hand in hand with doing something sustainable and good for our broader environment — and vice versa. This is a happy relationship I've tried to underline again and again in this book.

The most exciting thing about the natural link between saving money and being more environmentally responsible is that you only have to focus on one of them to achieve both. It's killing two (metaphorical!) birds with one stone. So you can play to your strengths. Some people find money *per se* a distasteful goal, worry about being perceived as cheap or just aren't hardwired to save. Yet deep down they know they need to get their bank balance on track. Well, much of that will come purely from embracing a greener approach to life — something they may be more than happy to do. One kind of green will automatically take care of the other. In the same way, some people are keen to change their habits for the good of the planet but keep putting it off. But when they see that so many of these habits can also be expressed in terms of financial gain, they'll be going green without even thinking about it!

Whatever your relationship with money or Earth happens to be, the two-way link between financial saving and taking care of the planet is something we all have working in our favour. My job, then, is not only to show you a variety of practical methods and principles to make your bank balance as healthy as it can be — whether you're unemployed, working a shop floor or a top executive. It's also to keep pointing out why a given money-saving strategy is also a planet-saving strategy. And you'll have every opportunity to come at things from the 'green' side of the equation if that's your preference.

Remember, we're soon going to have to start paying the true cost of any unsustainable behaviour — whether we like it or not.[1] Government regulations around the world are going to see to that over the next few years. So, life is likely to get significantly more expensive. That's just one more reason to start saving up more cash in the bank — and cut out those Earth-bashing habits as much as possible.

So, after being hit by a pandemic that gave us a financial scare but also taught us that we're able to (and should continue to) adjust our lifestyles, isn't this the perfect moment to learn the art of saving money in ways that just happen to be impactful?

---

1. I'm referring here to things like increased flight taxes, vehicle carbon taxes and deposits on re-usable bottles.

Why Me? Why Now?

Some people have a talent for sports; others can sing, dance, say witty things off the cuff or turn on the charm. My skill's nothing like as sexy as any of those: I'm just good at saving money. Ask the average career accountant how many eyes they've seen light up when they tell dates of their profession. Looking after pennies isn't a show that fills stadiums.

Kids screw up their faces when their parents tell them to save their pocket money wisely. Ebenezer Scrooge was a subject of satire for a reason. Actively saving — somewhat paradoxically in a money-crazed world — has always been a habit ripe for mockery. At best, the idea of getting good at it is just a yawn. Bean-counting makes you boring.

But what if you could stretch money without even thinking about it? What if it was just happening in the background of a fun and fulfilled life? Like you had some magic touch?

You wouldn't say no to the extra cash, would you?

And that's kind of what happened to me.

For a very long time, I didn't even know I had a 'gift' for saving. Until then, I was too busy working extremely modest jobs (or not at all), mostly failing to invest anything, travelling the world and indulging in luxury hobbies like motorsport and golf. But then, as my fourth decade began, I did a double-take at the five-figure balance in my savings account and asked myself, 'How did *that* happen?'

I began to think about what I had done right to reach such a happy state of affairs. For another several years, those thoughts did no more than bubble around my head. I didn't need to write them down, because I had the instinct within me.

Then COVID-19 struck. And I witnessed an explosion of fear around me.

People were flipping out about losing their jobs, their futures and the wellbeing of some supposedly essential machine called 'the global economy'. I was supposed to be losing my mind along with everyone else: I was 40 and effectively unemployed, selling only a handful of books each day. And there was no indication that things were going to change on that score. Yet I'd never felt more financially serene. I felt immune to the panic.

It was all down to that five-figure balance. Through 20 years of modest, intermittent labour I had amassed enough liquid money (not shares that had gone to junk!) to live for several years without lifting a finger. I was debt-free. And judging by the general panic, I was in the minority there. It was a surprise to discover that I'd saved tens of thousands of Euros more than peers who were earning multiples of what I was banking. The proverbial rainy day had come, and I found that I had apparently prepared for it best. Without even trying.

You're still thinking 'this guy's a developer or a lawyer,' right? Again, no. Writing isn't a side project for me. I'm an author, editor and journalist by trade. I've done a bit of PR and marketing too. These are not, and have never been, among the high-paying professions. Other jobs I've done, some of them well into my thirties? Golf caddie, truck driver, leaflet dropper, waiter, barman, cleaner of retirement homes, packer-of-magazines-into-boxes. I've even worked as a clown and a Spiderman impersonator. I tried starting a business — and had total revenues of about €45. All things considered, I've always been terrible at *making* money.

I was also quite good at spending it. Those costly hobbies aside, I'd taken in over 75 countries on my travels. I had, by a lot of measures, been signing cheques more liberally than most. If you're thinking 'that can't possibly add up' then you're not alone. Part of me was still thinking that too.

So if I had €50,000 in the bank after all that, it had to be because I really was, on some level, an ace saver.

Only now that the coronavirus had come to town did I get the impetus I needed to spell out the mechanics of what that ace saving had involved. Because that's when it really hit home just how many people had failed to lay any kind of liquid nest egg for a crisis like this. This was the moment I thought, 'Maybe I *should* write all of this down…'

But as I contemplated the relentlessly clear lockdown skies and breathed in the cleanest air my generation had ever enjoyed, I felt like this project shouldn't only be about the numbers. Because as some shelves went bare and birdsong replaced the groan of traffic as my morning alarm call, I felt compelled to make real changes in my own life. I took it upon myself to 'shop local' with immediate effect. I was going to think long and hard about future flying. And I knew there was zero chance I would ever own a car again.

Like much of humanity, I had truly woken up to the damage 'normal' was doing. But most of us were just going to go back to our old ways the moment we had the chance, weren't we? Could I help prevent that slide by showing people the raw financial benefits of more responsible behaviour? And conversely, could I use the 'in' topic of sustainability to sell the dull, derided one that is effective saving?

With this in mind, I began to boil my hitherto instinctive saving behaviour down into a fundamental strategy others could understand. This done, I examined how it could be applied to specific 'use cases' in everyday life. Finally — as I had suspected — I was able to note how doing so almost always represented a sustainable or impactful lifestyle choice too.

This book is the result of that analysis.

So now it doesn't matter if saving isn't in your blood the way it's in mine — the pages ahead are a practical manual for getting it right. As you'll see, saving is easy to learn. And so too, by extension, is doing your part to save this planet from going into meltdown!

It will be like running a marathon for charity: you're raising funds whilst doing good! But you can run this race without the pain in your legs. It's just training. The only thing you have to develop is your mindset and willpower. Soon, with the added motivation that you're living more responsibly than ever before, these will bed in and become habit. You'll forget the marathon entirely — until you check your bank account a few years later. At that point, you'll be rewarded with the same deep and lasting satisfaction long-distance athletes know so well.

Not just because of the numbers on your screen. But because it was a race well run.

What This Book Isn't

I've tried to keep this book short, sweet and a million miles away from the evangelical **bolds** and CAPITALS of the 'self-help' genre. When I read some of what's out there, I feel like I'm at a gospel church, listening to some television preacher transforming lives.

Maybe I'd sell more books that way, but it's not *my* way. I'm from South Africa and I'm not going to try and sound like I'm booming out my message from the top-left quarter of the world map. I hope to be read across the globe, and as such I'm expecting you to be absolutely anywhere. I'll write in British English, and to make a change from the usual assumption that we all live our lives in Dollars, I'll be using Euros as my reference currency. I did pen this book in Austria, after all.

I'm not in this because I plan to tour the world's auditoriums, basking in the grateful applause of audiences whose lives I've changed. (Though I don't completely loathe the thought!) And I *will not* have my teeth artificially whitened and appear on the cover of this or any other book. I cling to the noble idea that worthwhile advice should be able to sell itself.

Nor do I want to try and sound like some sentimental buddy who's going to put their arm around you and 'walk you through' your escape from credit card debt or the dark, scary world of money. I'm going to treat you as an intelligent person. Because if you're interested in sustainability and the bigger picture of the world you live in — regardless of your savings record — then clearly you're smart enough not to be patronised. Anyway, I'm not a qualified expert. The only impressive pieces of paper I can wave in your face are my bank records. (Is there such a thing as a degree in personal money-saving anyway?) I'm just a regular guy sharing what's worked for him in the past and what makes sense to him for the future.

And to return to the brevity thing: I don't wish to stretch out a simple two-hour read into a six-hour one by means of lengthy, made-up anecdotes beginning with 'Rachel was 42 and had hit rock bottom…'

So there won't be an inspiring, against-the-odds story here. I *didn't* come back from a place of loss and hopelessness. I'm not going to tell you I know what it is to be in debt and to have a bank balance mired in the red. Nobody has ever threatened to break my kneecaps for defaulting. No such excitement to report — I'm boring, stock standard and bang average! My parents paid for a university education, and thanks to an aunt's birthday contributions I had a couple of hundred Pounds in a British bank account before I graduated. So yeah, I was debt-free and had half a month's rent to my name when I took my first mildly serious job (hotel waiter) at 21. As near to square as makes no difference.

I know a lot of people take debt with them into their working lives, so I was lucky in that regard. Equally, however, I've yet to inherit a dime.[1] That one aunt aside, I've never even gotten money for my birthdays. I've done unspectacular, unremarkable jobs (in wage terms, at least — being a sports journalist was cool!) to earn pretty much every penny currently in my bank account.

Nope, they're never going to make a Hollywood movie out of me! I didn't come from behind like a tenacious boar, but nor was I ever thrashing around in a bathtub full of silver spoons. My story is simply one of making the numbers stack up from beginning at roughly zero. Without spectacular investments, endowments or a winning lottery ticket worth in excess of single digits. Whilst doing everything I ever wanted and more. All I can do is try and sum up the habits and thinking that have kept the numbers in my account showing a healthy, ever-growing green at the same time.

(While it's true that I have no specific experience of debt, I believe what I'm about to share will help those in the red towards a healthy bank account as much as it will anybody else.)

Like I said before, this book is a retrospective recognition of stuff that has worked and continues to work. I'm not going to tell you I had a strategy all along; some winning formula that I developed in my teens and now makes me look clever. Because it wasn't like that. I've bumbled through life like everyone else, getting a lot wrong and a few things right. Saving well appears to be one of the things I happened to do right.

With that out the way, here are a few more things I want to straighten out about what this book is *not*.

It's *not* about budgeting. By which I mean I'm not going to be breaking down your monthly expenses and telling you where it's all going wrong. Nor how to stop yourself stealing from yourself by transferring a portion of your salary to savings accounts you can't get at. That stuff is negative, and this book is about saving positively. So that having a 'budget spreadsheet' never needs to cross your mind. It certainly never crossed mine — which is a good thing considering I have no Excel skills whatsoever!

It's *not* about investing your money, compound interest (high school maths nightmares right there!) nor 'making it work for you' so that you're fabulously wealthy by 40. There are other books for that — not to mention any number of over-rated brokers. What this book *can* do, however, is put you in a position where you have some money to invest in the first place.

It's *not* a (direct) recipe for making millions. It's about making the most of what you *do* earn. Unless you're earning millions, you're obviously not going to save millions either. But the point of this book is to show that whatever humble sum you *can* save, it's more than you think. Which should, pretty soon, add up to a total that gives you options beyond staggering to the next payday. And these options *will* include a realistic start on the road to making millions — whether that's investment, starting a business or something else.

Likewise, it's *not* about showing you the way to a higher-paying job. Thinking back on my work as a journalist, print magazine editor and writer, it occurs to me that my annual salary peaked about a decade ago. Which should tell you that giving career advice isn't my forte. Each of us needs to figure out whether we really value regular pay rises and 'career progression', but this book is indifferent to the answer: it's about maxing out whatever you *do* earn. It's here to encourage even those of us with extremely average wages that we too can wake up to a tidy bank balance not long into our years of toil. Anyway, earning six figures doesn't mean you're going to save more than the person making your coffee. Just look at Harry Selfridge.

It's *not* about working your ass off and doing overtime. Quite the contrary. Society implies that hard slog is how you get more money in the bank, but the point of this book is to show that there's another way to get the same effect. If you can halve the funds you *thought* you needed to get through the month, then you can *also* halve your salary. And if you can do *that*, you could now be a part-timer working 2.5 days a week! That would mean time and choices — which could then be as modest or ambitious as you like. If you're a family type, you could spend that time with your loved ones — and that's valid! If you want an easy life, you could spend that time lazing around and enjoying seeing less of the boss — that's valid too! If you want to think and learn, you could spend that time reading — also valid! You could even learn higher-paying skills that will further reduce your work hours and/or bring your salary back up to where it was. And if you're entrepreneurial or serious about getting rich, you could spend that time on starting your own business or investing — another valid option!

As you're suspecting after the last two points, it's *not* about a traditional model of aspiration and ambition. Not the variety your teachers and parents and company bosses like to preach. But aspiration to stay out of debt and travel more without working harder? Aspiration to have more free time or be an entrepreneur? Ambition to write books, learn languages or try to be a professional golfer? These are the kinds of ambitions and aspirations that kept *my* inner Scrooge going — what are yours? Let's draw a clear distinction between *those* kinds of life motivation (which society describes using words such as 'laziness', 'unambitious', 'unrealistic' or 'dreamer') and the more traditional, socially approved definitions: study hard to land that degree, get more promotions, keep the pay rises coming, buy your own home (which isn't *really* yours, because the bank owns it...). Do you notice how 'normal' ambitions are all things that tie you down and keep you coming back for more time on the hamster wheel? A good saver looks beyond the goddamn wheel. He or she sees that our 'standard model' of aspiration has a way of ensuring that the moment you crest a hill, there's always another 'even more rewarding' one to aim at. Until you wake up one day and find you're too old to climb. There are other ways to a fun life and good finances than simply following the well-trodden path to more earnings. It's an insidious road that you can only survive with a degree of masochism and the regular purchase of shiny treats (which tend not to be Earth-positive items) that you *think* justify the whole thing.

Most critically of all, this book is *not* about all-consuming deprivation. There is *obviously* a relationship between saving and self-denial — just as there is between working late nights at the office and self-denial! — but thinking they're inevitably linked is a fallacy I'm here to destroy. The idea that substantial savings progress means a miserable life is nothing but a dangerous excuse for financial failure. One that keeps people buried in debt and scares them away from even trying. I feel so strongly about it that I'm going to finish by underlining the extent of the fun I had on my road to a financially secure COVID-19 experience.

So let me stress once more that I *did* drive racing cars for a period of three years in my 20s, regularly spending upwards of €1000 on a *single day* of fender-bashing at Donington Park or wherever. That was a solid two-thirds of my take-home wage. And I *did* have a golf club membership for two years after that, by which time I didn't have a job at all. These rich-man hobbies were the *opposite* of deprivation. They were reckless and inconceivable even for peers earning more than me, which nearly all of them were. Add to that the fact that I kept on travelling the world like a lunatic, including such frivolities as weddings, golf tournaments and bicycle races on different continents from that on which I lived.[2] Contrary to the popular image of the miser shivering on the sofa all day, I feel I've lived way more than most. All possible, I'm convinced, exactly because I've balanced the fun stuff out with hard-core savings. I've been open to economies other people don't consider, and that has allowed me to be carefree and indulgent in other ways.

But enough about me! It's time we dived into how *you* can save money. And the planet. And have a blast doing it.

---

1. I thought that was set to change when a lonely uncle died a decade ago, only to discover that in one final thrust of bitterness towards humanity he'd left his estate to the Society for the Prevention of Cruelty to Animals.
2. My pastimes weren't very 'green' back then — no question! Older and wiser, I'm trying to make up for that now. But the point here is just that they were expensive.

How This Book Works

The rest of this volume is a practical guide to ways in which you can change your behaviour or lifestyle choices to cut both your costs *and* your impact on the planet. Mostly, the emphasis will be on the money-saving aspect, though on some occasions I'll lead with the environmental positives — particularly in the 'Things and Stuff' chapter. Either way, I'll always aim to show you how each change is a win on both fronts.

Right after this section, I'll get into Dalkey's Law. This is the guiding philosophy — the one to which I gave barely any conscious thought for so many years — that got me to a sound financial position when COVID-19 hit. A fundamental mindset that will help you execute and build on nearly all of what follows in the book. Namely two specific savings strategies and then (divided into five themed chapters) a whole stack of concrete, real-life action points.

Not every last one of these will be relevant to you — nor am I claiming to cover absolutely everything. (I already have several pages of notes for the sequel!) I'm totally expecting these ideas to inspire you to more of your own. Ones that fit snugly with your priorities and the way you live — or *want* to live — your life.

You don't have to do everything in this book. Some of my tips are big and serious, while others are small and fun to the point where you might think I'm kidding. But I'm never kidding. Everything I'm going to mention has a more substantial impact (in both senses of the word) over the long term than people suspect. Still, just to help you prioritise, I'll sum up each section with a one-liner on the single most savings-effective change you can make. I've called this the '#1 TAKEAWAY'.

You'll also find a fun, illustrative calculation at the end of each section. This is where I show you the maths of how much you can save over a period of 19 years with just one tweak to the way you do things. The actual numbers are just educated examples — reality will vary depending on several factors, including your location. They're only there to get you thinking. And to remind you, over and over, of how small gains can add up to astronomical ones when you zoom out to the bigger picture.

To avoid accusations of sensationalism, I've gone with highly conservative figures for these example calculations. Yet in every case, it's astounding how much extra money you would find in your bank account at the end of those 19 years. One quick spoiler, because I can't resist: giving up your daily €1 bottle of spring water will be worth *almost €7000*.

You don't even want to know the numbers you get when you start to add the savings from each section together...

Why 19 years? Well, it's a long enough period to see significant cumulative effects play out...but it also happens to be the time that passes between the ages of 21 and 40. Twenty-one is probably when most of us begin to earn any significant money and/or take care of all our own bills. And 40 is halfway through the average lifespan and career. It's a good time to target having some significant capital in the bank. At 40, you're still young enough to do something useful with it.

40 is also the age at which I wrote this book, shortly after COVID-19's appearance on the scene. And as you already know, this project started with me want to unravel how my bank account got to where it was at that point.

So, to keep on underlining the tangible, long-term effect any small change to everyday behaviour will have, I've labelled the results of the 19-year calculations 'bank credit by 40.' But don't be thrown by what is only an illustration — this book is for all ages. It's never too late or too early to start reaping the benefits of good saving habits!

Also at the end of each section, I'll spell out the primary ways in which the change in behaviour concerned is also positively impactful in sustainability terms. A lot of the time the consequences are so obvious I barely need to mention them. (I mean, the ecological benefits of not buying water in plastic bottles aren't exactly a head-scratcher…) So feel free to let your imagination go wild at the further possibilities.

Where my impact notes are concerned, I'm going to assume you agree with me that construction, manufacturing and shipping are inherently undesirable things we should aim to reduce. I'm going to suppose you're on my page with the idea that while recycling is good, not making something at all is even better. That shipping can never be entirely clean, so let's cut it where we can. That forests are better than concrete jungles. That sourcing things locally, and supporting those who do the same, is a good practice made even better by the ongoing possibility of lockdowns and border closures. Oh, and that the quickest win when it comes to energy challenges is to need less of the stuff.

Ultimately, it's up to you to decide which of the practical hints in this book make most sense for you. When you're thinking about that, remember that you can set an example with whatever behaviour you're going to change in your life. It may not matter whether other people save money as well as you're going to, but it's important that *everyone* starts seeing 'saving the planet' as something entailing positive benefits for themselves. So if you can't do everything I'm going to mention, I encourage you to pick a few things that your peers will notice and question. If you give them something to think about, and a handful even follow your lead, then you'll have done something really powerful.

Dalkey's Law

And so to my guiding philosophy. Simply put, it's the concept that preventing money from leaving your bank account is mathematically equivalent to filling it up and then emptying it out again. Or, if you prefer, that saving is as powerful for your wallet as earning plus spending is.

This is light years away from rocket science. I'm not claiming a breakthrough here. What I *am* doing is taking the trouble to spell out a truth that has somehow slipped beyond our sight.

The reason so many of us struggle to see this simple mathematical reality is mostly just the world in which we live. We're immersed in the 'earning plus spending' ethos. The one which keeps us going to work month after month, unthinking, unchallenging and chasing the next job or pay rise. School education, from an early age, is always about 'getting a job' and very little about life hacks, entrepreneurship, investment...or savings. And unless you're reading this in North Korea, you live surrounded by advertising for shiny clothes, electronics and toys you're going to need money to buy.[1]

We needn't begin a critique of all that here: I'm just pointing out that we're raised in that 'earn and burn' culture from a young age. And where the voice of the 'savings' culture does manage to get a word in, it's usually in the form of nagging parents — or teachers trying to explain compound interest. It can't engage us because it appears in passive, negative or onerous contexts. No wonder we never develop that 'active awareness' of the massively empowering mathematics I mentioned up top!

So let's say it again: your bank balance at any given moment in time (your 40th birthday, say) doesn't give a flying monkey's whether you 'made' a Euro or 'saved' a Euro. It's indifferent to whether you made €2, and spent one of them, or whether you only made €1 in the first place and cut out the spend. Though our world glorifies one strategy over the other — Mr €2 has status and stuff, and we're led to revere status and stuff — that number in our credit column is the same. Financially speaking, the journey is irrelevant. That Euro is either there or it's not. Bottom line.

So rarely is this idea explicitly stated that I'm going to write it down as an equation.

€2 Earned - €1 Spent = €1 = €1 Earned - €0 Spent

Maybe, if some economist hasn't gotten there first, we can call it Dalkey's Law.

I know it looks tempting to remove that zero from the equation entirely. After all, it's not making any mathematical contribution in this case. And school algebra taught you to do away with such things. But that would be killing the entire point of the formulation, which is to give that '€0 Spent' term the right to exist. The *explicit* spot consumer culture trains us not to see. We need our 'useless' zero, because without a slot for 'not spent', we're going to forget that 'not spent' is a valid option in real life. Which is a constant series of decisions (from tiny to momentous) about what you're going to spend *and* what you're going to *not* spend. The zero is critical to the purpose of the Dalkey's Law equation: to remind us that 'not spending' can logically be taken as seriously as 'earn and burn'. That 'not spending' has an active influence on any person's financial outcomes.

If the equation has helped you accept the last two statements in the paragraph above, then I'm more than happy to bundle up those statements and move on with them. No more maths.

Dalkey's Law Gigs

It's not only our aspirational culture that tries to make us forget the tangible power of 'not spending'. There's also a certain well-documented feature of human psychology: we like to see cause and effect unfold before our eyes. We don't process the effects of 'not doing something' nearly so well. Particularly if those effects play out over months, years and decades.

Given this, what if we could frame the whole 'not spending' deal in a more natural way? What if we could see it as positively causing an effect? That would be a powerful tool when it comes to decision-making time, particularly if we're easily tempted.

I think there *is* a way. I'm going to do what your teachers and parents never did: introduce the concept of time spent saving as *paid work*. We have no trouble seeing an hour working for €20 as a trade of our time for money in the bank, right? Yet if we spend an hour to ensure that we *don't spend* €20 (eg. by repairing some-thing ourselves, shopping around for better deals or taking the time to buy something second hand) we classify this as a different sort of activity. But why? Both approaches are *exactly the same thing*: an exchange of our time for money in the bank!

Both strategies are short paid assignments. In current economic parlance, it seems appropriate to call them 'gigs'. But since everyday language completely fails to give us words to describe the second variety as such, I'm going to provide some. I'm going to call what that hobby repairer or smart shopper does a 'Dalkey's Law Gig'.

So now you're going to know what I'm talking about when I use that term throughout this book. It will describe scenarios in which taking time, trouble or a mildly tough decision are (contrary to the popular narrative) rewarding you financially.

Dalkey's Law Gigs in the Real World

Beyond the confines of this book, potential Dalkey's Law Gigs can be tricky for the untrained eye to spot. Even when you do see them, external factors have a habit of getting in the way. Here's an example from the complex, tricky world of real life.

Flagging a taxi from an airport is one of the fastest ways, on a per-minute basis, to make your money disappear. The first time I noticed people doing it, at London Heathrow when I was 21 and earning minimum wage, I had an instinctive reaction that has left its mark. How could folks be so *rich*? Pound coins were literally flying out of the window every few metres they drove! Didn't they know there was a bus alternative that was as good as free?

On any given day, at any busy airport, hundreds of people grab a taxi when they 'just want to get home' and can't be bothered with the negligibly priced but slower public transport. Let's say Tom is a highly paid office worker. Tom spends €50 on that late evening airport taxi in order to get to bed an hour earlier. All so that he can get up in the morning, go to work and earn...€50 an hour.

Now let's say you're the sort of person who feels instinctively drawn to that €1.50 bus. You're on minimum wage. And Tom is your travel companion. He might be a friend, family or an acquaintance.

When you say you're waiting for that bus that takes an hour longer to get home, Tom may very well roll his eyes and call you an unflattering name. But mathematically speaking, you're just achieving the same result in a different way. Because you know Dalkey's Law and see its broader implications. In this case, that an hour's time spent to *save* €50 is as financially useful to you as an hour's time spent *earning* €50. You see a Dalkey's Law Gig in front of you.

But then we come to that real-world context. Tom will have his €50 back by the end of his first hour's accounting or lawyering the next day. The sheer rate of his regular earnings makes that taxi fare pale into insignificance. An hour's wage is neither here nor there when he's got a salary calculated on 40 hours a week. Tom can 'afford' it, as they say.

Now, how does this apply to you and your decision, especially in the face of his teasing? Dalkey's Law still holds for both, but in practice we must consider that *Tom's* €50 isn't the same as *your* €50. He sees it as small change. But for you and me, average people of more modest means? €50 is serious money. Money that takes anything up to several hours to earn.

I think most low earners instinctively recognise that inequality. But what they *rarely* do is make the jump to seeing this as an *opportunity*! To see that given their financial circumstances, this is a moment to grab a lucrative Dalkey's Law Gig with both hands. That for one exciting hour they'll actually be on level pegging with big-earning Tom! That this is a rare chance to gain (ie. *not lose*) more in a single hour than they will in any other hour in the week to come.

It's clearly *not* about winning some contest with Tom — but perhaps using the big earner as a small-scale reference helps you see the real prize more clearly. The real prize being, of course, an additional €50 in your bank account.

People struggle to see this real prize (and the opportunity to grab it) because the results of their decision aren't immediately apparent. Short-term, you might have a chilly wait at the bus stop, then a jerky midnight ride through deserted and depressing suburbs. But when you look a little further, of course, you see that you're starting the week on zero rather than -€50. All other things being equal for the week, then, you'll have *€50 more in your bank account* at the end of it. It's a Dalkey's Law Gig, plain and simple. But it plays out slowly. It doesn't feel or look like anything. And it's never going to be as seductive as a warm taxi!

If there's literally a 0% chance of you taking the taxi, then you can't really frame this as a Dalkey's Law Gig, since there's no 'spend' option with which to compare the bus ride. But if the taxi is ruled out on principle, then you don't need this chapter at all — you're clearly already good at saving! You probably already see how your prudent spending habits are going to add up over the years.

For the rest of us, there's a decision to take. And while the maths is simple, real life rarely is. We're people, not robots! We might be tempted into the taxi because we're tired or emotional or lazy or sick of Tom's chirping. The moment there's any chance we'll succumb, clinging to the idea that we're effectively *getting paid* to heave that suitcase or wait in the cold for an hour becomes extremely helpful. It's like being offered overtime at an extraordinary rate! If your fatigue still outweighs the overtime benefit, fair enough. But be aware of the gig on offer, at least.

As you've already seen with Tom, other people (and partners, I'm afraid to say) are a recurring problem. *You* grasp what's at stake, but *they* will try to lead you astray. People mock, people persuade, people cajole, people make faces, people yawn grumpily, people throw false logic around, people say, 'oh, come on, it's only €25 if we share!' And they may not be impressed when you point out that, quite apart from money, having a car to yourself is a selfish indulgence from an emissions perspective.

Other people don't get the maths like you do. They will question you making a smart earnings decision now, late at night, but not why they themselves get up for work in the morning (still yawning grumpily!) in order to sacrifice their time for money in a more socially approved fashion they accept as a fact of life. They'll frame your hour on the bus as some kind of masochistic self-denial, yet refuse to see that their going to work on any given day is much the same thing. Each is a case of denying yourself free time in exchange for money, is it not?

People will bring their best powers of persuasion, but it's when you stand your ground in these moments of temptation that you can really start to consider your saving as €50 in your bank account that you wouldn't otherwise have. Make a habit of standing your ground, and you have €50 amounts that will start to tally up to something really juicy over time.

For another good illustration of a realistic Dalkey's Law Gig you can get on holiday, let's talk camping for a moment. Even if you pay for a campsite in which to put up your tent, it will almost certainly be cheaper than a hotel or Airbnb, right? Everyone knows this. But everyone *also* knows there's more work (and dirt) involved in putting up a tent than wandering through the door of a clean apartment — and that's enough to end the discussion for 95% of us. But the other 5%? They say, 'If I skip the hotel, I'm getting paid €20 or €30 to walk a few extra steps to the shower and shake down a tarp in the morning. Hell, that's the easiest money I'll ever make!'[2]

Some Dalkey's Law Gigs can even be seen as generating passive income. If you spend, say, three hours on figuring out a telephone billing option that will save you €20 a month *ad infinitum*, then you're getting limitlessly paid for that time investment! Who says no to a gig like that?

Once again, there's no revolutionary maths here. It's just about putting a positive spin on the deal. When we reframe saving as earning, it's a lot easier to see the plus side. It's a lot easier to set the time aside for the task in question. Just like we do when we take a job, in fact.

Time is Money

To apply Dalkey's Law effectively in real life, the smart saver must always be able to see how much they're saving and, often, how much of their time that's worth. Self-employed people have a very good idea of the latter, but it's a much simpler calculation for employed people. You can do it in 20 seconds. Yet because wages are guaranteed and regular, not many salaried staff can rattle off their hourly earnings without stopping to think about it. If that's you, it's time to do some quick sums. What's your take-home salary? How many hours do you put in every month? That's all you need.

Knowing your hourly worth helps you make decisions all the time. In the taxi example, it does two crucial things. One, it tells you whether you're one of the Toms or not.[3] Two, it puts that 'overtime offer' into perspective. Not accepting an hour's inconvenience to save €50, and then going to work for €10 an hour the next day, would be a strange logic indeed.

You also need your hourly earnings number to see when a saving *isn't* worth the time. For me, thinking about what I could make in an hour is the reason I don't take loyalty cards or collect air miles, for example. I could write whole chapters in the hours I spend hunting down forgotten passwords, deleting junk emails, fighting to have my miles recorded and fiddling with coupons. A few years ago, I decided spending my time writing books like this would earn me more than loyalty schemes would save me.

Dalkey's Law and Denial

Dalkey's Law Gigs can play out in an infinite number of ways. It isn't always as simple (or cold) as freezing at bus stops or getting muddy feet for longer-term financial gain. The process itself might just as easily turn out to be healthy, relaxing, educational or enjoyable. It could be the impetus to give up smoking. It might give you the lazy days you've unconsciously been denying yourself. Perhaps you'll learn how to repair something you couldn't before. It could mean reading more. It could mean an extra holiday at the end of the year.

Because it's worth repeating: I'm not here to make you suffer through constant denial. I'm the guy who spent all those saved taxi fares on blasting around racetracks and muddling about in Mongolia! I've seen how saving on the boring, mundane, easy stuff can free up money for exciting, amazing stuff. The trick is to know when it's time for a treat and when it's not. If everything you do is a treat, that's not a strategy.

Sure, denial plays its part in Dalkey's Law Gigs *at times*. Nobody expects you to love every moment of a 'traditional' gig, so why should this be any different? But like I said before, it's a long way from an all-consuming imperative. And a little denial is something you need to deal with *anyway* if you want to live a more constructively sustainable life.

Moreover, many 'denials' will, in fact, turn out to be blessings in themselves! There's an odd satisfaction in discovering that you didn't actually *need* to buy so many shoes, eat so much steak or travel abroad every month. It's the pleasure that goes with learning to value the fundamental things in life. Didn't we all experience a little of that feeling during our respective COVID-19 lockdowns?

When these things we think of as 'denial' turn out not only to save us money and Earth as we know it, but to actually be unexpected pleasures too, then is there really even a choice to make?

Speaking of blessings and pleasures…yes, living by Dalkey's Law *could* also mean doing less 'regular' work, if that's your priority. We only need to take the gig principle a step further to see how every time we actively cut a cost — especially where that saving is repeatable and regular — then it's the easiest slice of steady self-employment you can pick up. Saving €50 a week is €50 you don't need to go and earn. Moreover, you get paid immediately and there's no tax! If all of that adds up to fewer hours reporting to an office, and more hours to do what you want (again, it could be anything from pure sloth to founding your startup), then I'm having a hard time seeing the downside.

Nobody is saying you can hand in your notice tomorrow. Everyone's skills and numbers are different. And unless an aunt has conveniently left you her life's savings, nearly all of us need *some* income — we do need to put food on the table. But if you work to ingrain Dalkey's Law into your mindset, you'll be able to see gig opportunities most people are too stuck in the rat race, too blinded by the wider narrative, to notice.[4]

It's a safe bet that if you just think of saving not as the lame, sickly sibling of 'earn and burn', but rather as a healthy twin with exactly the same mathematical clout, you'll land up *at least* as rich as peers earning far more — and often working harder — than you are. And because you're embracing more 'not spending' options — which play out at home and on your own terms — chances are you're more relaxed and happier too!

#1 TAKEAWAY Think of any time spent saving money as time spent doing paid work.

---

1. For an entertaining yet thought-provoking perspective on the post-World War II explosion of consumer culture in the United States, read *The Life and Times of The Thunderbolt Kid* by Bill Bryson.
2. At the risk of stating the obvious, we're assuming for the purposes of this example that going on holiday and paying for accommodation of *some* description is a given. Clearly, staying at home would be the cheapest option of all.
3. If you are, please note that I'm open to artistic grants...
4. One example of a Dalkey's Law Gig that only occurred to me when I became a freelancer is that of a skills exchange. I did it with this very book: instead of paying my editor, I did an edit-swap in which she looked over my manuscript and I looked over her blog posts. Instead of each earning money we could use to pay other people, we just each gave each other our time and understood that the value came in the form of cash *not leaving* our bank accounts. The outcome was exactly the same as each of us sending and paying invoices, only without the hassle and tax! You obviously don't need to be a freelancer to pick up on this variation on saving, even if it's only once a month on a Saturday morning.

Two Rules To Live By

Zone in on Free

A bit of an obvious one, this!

Clearly, prioritising free stuff (whether goods, services or activities) is a great way to help your bank balance swell rather than sink. But that doesn't mean people don't overlook this fact *all the time* — and then wonder where their cash went.

Every time we do something free instead of something that costs, we're applying Dalkey's Law. We may not be adding to our bank balance, but we're stopping it from dropping. When it all comes out in the wash down the line, it'll count for the same.

When we make plans with friends, how often do we forget that we could simply meet up outside instead of sitting down and spending money on food and drink we might not even want? Unless you live in a very unfortunate part of the world, there are bound to be parks where you can throw a ball around, beaches or lakes inviting you to chill or pleasant strolls you can enjoy. And you can always bring a cheap picnic with you![1]

Granted, that's not going to work all year round unless you live in the tropics. And some of those outdoor ideas may not be so smart (or possible) after nightfall. But be proactive about taking these opportunities when you can. If your only option after dark is the local pub, then why not push for daytime meetups? There's really no shame in spending Saturday night at home when you've been sociable all day long.

When it comes to getting exercise, things like cycling, hiking, running or playing ball sports in the park are free apart from the odd initial equipment investment. (See also 'The Gym'.) There are any number of YouTubers ready to lead your morning yoga class for nothing.[2]

Commuting on foot or by bicycle is also as good as free over the long term. On the other hand, public transport and private cars cost money. Even if the bus fare to class or your job seems like small change every time, remember how it can add up. So too do longer-term tickets, *even* if we're talking about Vienna's €1-a-day annual card, which is as good a deal as you'll find anywhere.

Free is everywhere, if you're ready to look for it.

Are there certain days or nights when your local museums offer free entry? Do you need a cinema ticket when you can watch an awe-inspiring sunset? Can't you get most of the shopping experience by browsing without actually *buying* things? Why not do a spot of volunteering? It's a way to meet people, it's socially positive and — unlike the things you might do instead — won't cost a dime!

Speaking of social positivity, there are a few things I'm definitely *not* suggesting when I tell you to zone in on the free. Don't run out of restaurants without paying the bill. Don't leach off other people. Make a point of paying your personal debts. And just because ebooks, movies and music are easy to get for nothing doesn't mean you should do so — we artists also have rent to pay. And remember, karma's a bitch.

#1 TAKEAWAY Open your eyes to free (or much cheaper) ways to socialise with others than hanging in bars and restaurants.

- Cost of going for a walk or kicking a ball: €0
- Cost of light meal plus drink in café: €15
- Saving if one outing per week is kicking a ball instead of café: €15
- Available annual saving: €780
- Bank credit by 40: **€14,820**

IMPACT: Because human nature is to forget about doing the right thing when money's on offer, commercial transactions are inevitably tied up with *some* kind of not-so-green behaviour. The fewer commercial transactions you do, then, the more you squeeze that behaviour.

BONUS TIP: Avoid ever having to pay for a toilet by using one whenever it's available! Make the loo your last port of call before leaving restaurants, trains or airports, for example. Even if it doesn't seem so urgent at the time.

---

1. But remember, there are picnics and picnics. You care about the planet, so bring your own cups and cutlery, and avoid lazy supermarket options that come pre-packed in plastic. This kind of convenience is a huge part of why the environment is groaning under senseless waste.
2. Although I would completely understand if you'd rather support someone in your local community.

Milk Your Employer

Sounds harsh, doesn't it?

Well, so is overtime, being expected to answer emails on weekends and the boss constantly being too busy to talk about that pay rise. So unless you work for yourself or your family, or are utterly convinced that the people you work for treat you with saintly goodness in all things, start considering your job not just as a way to earn money, but also as a way to cut your life costs.

Sometimes we forget to take a holistic view of the advantages we can get from our employer. We fixate on our salary, when there's so much more. Are there worthwhile benefits you only need to fill out a form to get? Is there a subsidised cafeteria? A gym you could use for nothing?

Does the boss buy lunch once a month? That's not the day to pull a sickie! Maybe you don't like your colleagues and don't want to go to the Christmas party, but you could think of it as a Dalkey's Law Gig because there's financial credit in the form of a dinner's worth of groceries you don't have to buy. Spin it a little more, and it's like you're getting an appearance fee!

Even the small things will add up. Try to develop a taste for the office coffee because that Starbucks on the way from the station is not a long-term option. (See also 'Consider that Coffee'.) Charging your phone and other devices, or perhaps even your car, at work is energy you don't have to pay for at home. Is there a shower, and did anybody say it's only there for cyclists to use?[1] Everyone else is using the printer for their personal flight tickets, so don't be the mug running down to the print shop with a USB stick. Do you have a company phone with unlimited data? You could think about using it as a hotspot at home rather than paying for WiFi. And what's in the kitchen? I once worked at a company that provided free bread and peanut butter for the staff. (See also 'Peanut Butter Sandwiches'…)

Don't fall into the trap of feeling guilty. A lot of employers talk a good game about how everyone pulls for each other and your team is basically a big, happy family. But when push comes to shove, you're just a number on an accounting statement to them. When they need to save *their* expenses, I fear they won't keep you aboard just to be nice. (You may already have discovered that when COVID-19 hit.) So don't feel bad about using them to save on *your* expenses.

Speaking of which, grab every receipt on any work-related travels! I've actually had colleagues who don't bother to claim their expenses! Some may be mired in that guilt trap I just mentioned. Some have a tendency to write off money that they've already spent as irrelevant. Which, if all you have to do is fill out a form in order to cancel that outlay (without having to regurgitate that dinner you had), is clearly false thinking of the highest order. Considering you're already getting paid a salary for your form-filling time and then *also* get money back for the brief hassle, this is like a double-time Dalkey's Law Gig!

I'd even go so far as to say that sticking your hand up for lots of business trips is one of the best savings techniques available.[2] They get you out of the office and offer a change of scenery. Even if it's only for a day or two, that's a few meals your company should buy instead of you. And if the trip happens to be to an interesting place, you can tack on a holiday without paying the travel fares! The financial savings can seriously add up — and if doing that means you take one less flight in the year, so too do the carbon savings!

But the best time to get serious gains from your employer is before you even start. What perks can you negotiate before you sign? A company laptop that you're free to take home could save you several hundred Euros buying your own — and cloud storage enables you to keep your private files away from the boss. A company phone could save you three figures on device costs, even if you put your own SIM in the second slot to keep your affairs separate. And can you get a credit card so that the whole expense reclamation thing is no time and trouble?

Remember that once you've gotten as far as talking about these details with a company, your prospective employer is probably quite keen on you. Bear in mind too that hiring the right people is a pain for most firms, so don't buy into the idea that if you ask for too much they'll move onto the next person. It's a nasty consequence of our hamster-wheel society that we're so easily talked into that 'pay review in six months', which invariably disappoints. Rather get all your pay rises upfront. There's never going to be a better time to push!

#1 TAKEAWAY Grab every benefit you can from your employer — particularly items or services you'd otherwise pay for, such as laptops or phones.

- Approximate average cost of new personal laptop and phone every 5 years: €1200
- Bank credit by 40 if you get these from employers: **€4800**

IMPACT: A mixed bag. You can reduce waste by not doubling up on devices. And using the same flight for work and holiday would certainly reduce your carbon footprint.

---

1. This is one of those moments where you might think I'm kidding — but I've been known to take advantage of office shower facilities even when I've not ridden a bike to work. Getting in ultra-early to shower and dress at the office might mean beating rush hour, for example, saving emissions, time and annoyance as well as money. Or perhaps staying later and getting your evening scrub out of the way after work might mean getting a seat on an off-peak train instead of having to stand?

2. First prize, from an ecological perspective, is to convince your bosses that *nobody* takes the trip. That video calls might suffice. Only when you've lost that fight should you switch to being a keen volunteer!

Three Direct Debits You
Don't Need

The Phone Contract

If you haven't noticed that your phone provider is a mercenary, cynical, cunning operation bent on debiting your bank account for the rest of your life, then I suspect you've never read your bill too closely or tried to get out of your contract.

Mobile phone companies are your natural enemy, dear saver! Their *raison d'être* is to make it as easy as possible for you to spend money on a regular basis without really noticing.

Don't let them do it to you!

The key thing here is to examine prepaid options. There's every chance that you'll be able to slash your mobile costs in half — at least. Since I managed to wriggle out of my monthly deal in the middle of 2019 (better late than never!) and switched to buying prepaid credit, I'm spending €10 every three or four months rather than €10 every month.

I can't guarantee you're also going to spend 75% less on mobile expenses. It depends partly on the range of options available in your market. It also depends, to some extent, on how addicted you are to your phone and your discipline with regard to using

WiFi whenever it's available. What I can say with conviction is that it's one of the easiest ways I've found to make my life cheaper. With no discernible sacrifice.

Mobile phone contracts and deals — any relationship with a recurring monthly cost, basically — rely heavily on customers failing to notice some crucial truths. The first abomination to elude so many of us is that these arrangements goad us into buying more gigabytes, minutes and text messages than we can actually use in a month. Which would be just fine if those goods didn't arbitrarily 'expire' after that month, forcing us to buy them again. Think about how crazy that is. Data isn't like a banana — it doesn't *go* rotten! Why do we let mobile companies get away with this?

The second thing they catch us out with is the seductive promise of a new phone every two years or so. They make that 'upgrade' feel painless, even though you're paying for it every month. And the thing is, we don't *need* an upgrade every two years. It's wholly unnecessary for anybody willing to take basic care of their device. Beyond that, it fuels our throwaway culture and encourages tech companies to push on with their disgraceful, wasteful habit of building in obsolescence. When we let them get away with that, we're doing exactly the opposite of this book's title — we're spending more whilst destroying the planet!

Mobile companies also hope we're never going to spot that the way people use their phones has changed. That their 'deals' are based on an outdated model. With free, worldwide WhatsApp or Facebook calls now commonplace and acceptable for business, we can get by almost entirely without 'regular' network calls. WiFi is nearly everywhere, to the point where you'd have to make an active effort to use as much data as you did even a year or two ago. If you use WiFi and free communication apps wherever possible, do you seriously *need* 10 gigabytes a month? 120

minutes of network calls? *1000 SMS messages!?* When did texting your app-shy grandma and ringing the odd official number last get you anywhere near those limits?

These are just some of the reasons most deals make no sense anymore. And why you should be looking out for the chance to switch to using prepaid vouchers where the value *does not expire.* Ideally, they translate to good old pay-as-you-go credit, where you pay fractions of cents per call, text or data usage. It's less good if the voucher represents specific quantities of minutes, messages or data — in this case always judge the value on what's likely to run out first — but as long as there's no time limit on it and your discipline with regard to switching to WiFi is good, you're going to save money regardless.

Basic pay-as-you-go credit vouchers are still available in many countries. The cellular giants like to hide them, however, with some having gone so far as to abolish them entirely — they'd much rather force you to give them monthly money regardless of your usage, you see. Every country will vary, but looking beyond the traditional telco players could be the trick. Don't discount the post office or the corner shop. For me in Austria, it was as simple as switching to the service provided by Hofer, a supermarket chain. That's where I go to buy my €10 voucher every quarter-year or so.

I'll be first to admit that the research work is boring here. But this is a classic Dalkey's Law Gig — it's paid work! If the time you take comparing deals and rates yields a saving that recurs every month for years to come without you lifting a finger after the initial time investment, how can you say no? If that's not a good deal compared to your day job (which expects you to lift fingers all day long!), then I'm fascinated to hear more about your work!

Back to the prepaid, no-expiry-date credit I hope you're going to find. Yes, one consequence of 'paying as you go' is that you'll have to think more about when and how you use your phone. A few bytes here and there are negligible, but you might skip streaming an entire HD movie on the bus. And you could email companies rather than ringing them up. By avoiding the more costly aspects of mobile usage, you'll find your voucher seems endless. Again, it's a Dalkey's Law Gig: you're effectively *getting paid* to be patient for half an hour and watch that film on the WiFi at home!

Lastly, paying cash upfront for your mobile needs is a liberating step towards controlling your saving. In fact, any monthly direct debit you can eliminate from your life is a win. When companies no longer have the right to pillage your account at will, then you're in full control of your spending. Plus you'll never have to fight about your unexpected roaming bill with a chatbot again!

#1 TAKEAWAY Escape that contract and hunt down a way to pay only for what you use. Don't buy anything that 'expires'.

- Monthly mobile phone 'deal' costs: €15
- Available annual saving if you cut costs 50% with prepaid: €90
- Bank credit by 40: **€1710**

IMPACT: Ignoring deals 'including phone' as a matter of principle goes a little way to reducing electronic waste and the Earth-rape (remember the weird metals they mine to put in your handset!) that feeds it.

BONUS TIP: Be extremely cautious with 'convenient', all-in-one packages offering you mobile, television, home internet and a monthly back rub. Once you're invested, it's hard to isolate the individual parts — such as your phone spend — that could be cheaper. As for 'television', isn't pretty much all of it available on your laptop or tablet these days?

BONUS TIP: Having said you should wait to watch that movie on the WiFi at home, there's also the possibility that getting more mobile data could *replace* WiFi for you. It depends on network speeds, data costs and your expected usage. Take time to do the maths for where you live.

The Gym

Are you one of the thousands of people who, at the start of some year or other, resolve to Get Fit/Look Great/Both? And then pour cash into the greediest money drain known to humankind?

Everyone knows that most keen-eyed gym converts don't see it through. The story is all too familiar: the new recruit is there on time and ready to rock for the first week or three. And then...the holiday in Cuba, Jack's 30th, craziness at work, their daughter's illness. Legitimate reasons turn to excuses, and the habit fades away like the excess kilos were supposed to do.

This has not escaped the attention of the gyms, which is why they try to lock you into a contract when you're full of beans at the start. A deal so well sealed that you'll need a crack team of lawyers to crowbar yourself out of it.[1] Once you stop coming to the gym, your local fitness provider has hit business nirvana: people are transferring them money each month for nothing in return.

But contracts aside, there's another reason why paying for a gym is among the most preposterous and least justifiable ways to empty your pockets.

You can get exercise for free. Easily. Everywhere.

When I walk past window displays of people toiling away on stationary bikes at fitness studios, all wearing grimaces that suggest they're not doing this as part of an ironic comedy installation, I always want to wave my arms at them and gesture at the street outside in animated fashion. Don't they know that for the one-off investment of a bicycle, they can revolve pedals in fresh air for the rest of their lives without paying another dime? All that free tarmac is right in front of their noses, for crying out loud! How do they not *see* it?

I feel equally certain that treadmill people are on a steady diet of stupid pills. You get onto a machine that allows you to run whilst standing still. Excuse me? Yes, it bears repeating: they're paying money to make the road run underneath them, instead of them running along the road for free. In a stuffy, sweaty room, as opposed to outside in fresh air.

And nearly all of these people are wearing headphones. Which proves that it's not the beats coming over the gym speakers they're paying for.

Those whose goal is to tone and sculpt will hasten to point out that it's not all about the cardio. You want to use equipment too. I'm not going to drill down into the finer points of your exercise programme, but I'd urge you to at least *question* that assumption. Sit-ups and press-ups may not be part of your routine, but dozens of other exercises for every imaginable purpose can be done at home. If YouTube doesn't help you here, an hour or two with a personal trainer surely will. And that investment will cost nothing compared to a gym membership.

Gyms do have their place, I suppose. If you're a bodybuilder or a rugby player, and strong muscles are your game, then you may well need some of the more complex equipment you'll only find in a gym. If it's winter in a really cold country and you're training for a bike race somewhere sunny, then I get the static bike thing — I've tried February wind chill and it ain't fun. Likewise, I'd understand you using the heated pool for a few laps with that triathlon in Brazil coming up. But don't tell me you need a conveyor belt to run on when there's a free pavement outside. Please.

In the age of pedometers, pulse trackers, Fitbits and all manner of other ever-improving wearable measurement devices, ask yourself if you really need to pay a gym subscription. And if the answer is yes, do you genuinely need it all year round? If not, is there a cheaper way?

Remember, the gyms bank on you being lazy and you failing to do the maths. Don't play into their hands. Doing your sums isn't unpaid labour like it was in high school. It's another Dalkey's Law Gig that will put money in your bank!

#1 TAKEAWAY Cycle or run through your neighbourhood for free. Swim in the lake or river for free. Find out whether your local park has free equipment you can use. Learn exercises you can do at home.

- Cheap monthly gym membership: €15
- Available annual saving: €180
- Bank credit by 40: **€3420**

IMPACT: If we have fewer gyms, it means less construction, less manufacturing/shipping of machines and slimming our electricity consumption!

BONUS TIP: Get on YouTube. Not just for the hundreds of routines and classes you could find for when the weather is cold, but for the tips on creating home-made versions of the gym equipment you're currently paying for.

BONUS TIP: Start running or cycling to work and appointments. Kill the exercise and commuting birds with the same stone. See also 'Zone in on the Free' and 'Scrap the Car'.

---

1. Remember the *Friends* episode where Ross and Chandler tried to escape their gym deal? It's not so far from the truth...

Insurance

I've never agreed with doing grown-up things as default. The fact that most adults do something isn't a reason in itself. Sure, this is nothing more than a teenage mindset I never grew out of, but it has served my saving well. Never more so than when it comes to insurance.

Just to be clear, I'm not talking about 'insurance' of the kind that pays for a country's health care system, unemployment funds or pensions. These are communal goods that make life fairer and more civilised for all. I'm talking about insurance of a personal, voluntary nature.

To me, 'insurance' was always just some long word your parents mentioned when they reeled off all the reasons they weren't going to buy you a go-kart. Perhaps that sowed a seed. Because once I got old enough to understand what insurance was, I felt a clear, calm certainty that I didn't need it. I probably wasn't alone on this in my early 20s, when everyone's poor and feels indestructible. But now that I'm 40, I'm pretty sure I'm the last one not paying private insurance premiums for things like theft or houses falling down.

Like populist politicians, the insurance industry plays on our deepest fears and sells nothing but a tenuous peace of mind. Their 'product' sits snug and well with our control-freakish disconnection from the planet we live in, our faith in technology and the destruction of family and community. *I must be able to control everything*, we think. *Nobody else will help me when the worst happens*, we think. *Paying money to a company will cover that unhappy scenario*, we think.

These are powerful thoughts, but I believe we need to get a grip on ourselves and stop thinking we're so smart and indestructible. Most humans didn't *have* insurance until somewhere around your grandparents' time. From caveman prehistory until three or four centuries ago, it wasn't even a thing. How our ancestors would be puzzled by all of this safety-netting! But then they weren't nearly so full of themselves: they knew life hung by a thread. They knew a tornado, a rabid dog, a plundering tribe, a drought — yes, even a pandemic — could be the end of you at any moment. Bad things happened, and if they happened to you then that was just life. Unlucky. This was a cruel old planet.

They probably didn't have great expectations from the medical technology of the time either — but isn't that a peace of mind in itself? As much as modern medicine saves and cures, its nasty by-product is the notion that we're infinitely repairable as long as the costs are covered. The real truth, if you have that attitude, can often prove deflating to say the least.

The irony is that life is safer than ever before. Rabid dogs are hard to find. Plundering tribes have been all but eliminated. Even COVID-19 has only nabbed a fraction of the global population. And yet no matter how much further the odds go in our favour, we'll obsess all the more about that ever-shrinking chance of a calamity we can't control. The media feeds our minds by pasting the worst on every front page. We see news of the worst-case scenario all the time, and start to think it's more common than it actually is. Governments, meanwhile, feed those 'what-if' thought patterns by making things like car insurance compulsory. The private sector rides on the same train (pet insurance? Seriously?).

Maybe it's just that I'm from Africa, where life is cheap and the general vibe is to take a somewhat fatalistic view of the sanctity of our own health and existence, but I'm actually at peace with the idea that a tornado might pull my house down or that I might be involved in a serious accident. If it costs money, I simply expect to pay for it. This isn't revolutionary thinking — it's the whole of history before insurance was invented. The wonder is that half the world has forgotten it so fast.

But even if you can't make peace with the ages-old idea that we live on a planet where capricious and random events of an unwanted nature can occur, and even if you don't want to focus on a healthy, two-way support network as your 'safety net', and even if you don't think it's odd to pay for something you hope never to need, then consider the raw maths.

Let's say you pay €10,000 in insurance premiums over a number of years. An alternative (given a tiny bit of discipline) is to put *the same* €10,000 into your savings account.

Let's look first at paying €10,000 in premiums. Now, because bad things don't *actually* happen very often, you're unlikely to ever claim from your insurance. So you've wasted your money. If you *do* ever claim, then it will on average be for less than you have paid in over the years. (Insurance companies would go out of business if their computers didn't make sure that was the case.) And that's if your insurers pay out at all. Nobody loves catching you out on a technicality more than your insurer.[1] That's why I said the 'peace of mind' they sell you is tenuous. It may be no more than an illusion.

Scenario two? Well, probably nothing bad ever happens to you. And if it does, you have €10,000 waiting in a bank account! Where it earned interest, so it's actually now *more* than €10,000. And this is an all-purpose insurance that always pays out without question — you can use it for hospital, unemployment, replacing stolen cars, anything you want! No claim forms required. No increased premiums. And no arguments: you'll find the person dealing with your claim remarkably pleasant, in fact.

There's absolutely nothing wrong with contributing to your own emergency fund. Knowing that this is all there is will actually help your savings discipline like nobody's business.

And it's worth underlining the key benefit one last time: you still *own and control* that money. So what happens when you *do* get that big job, win the lottery or save so well that €10,000 is neither here nor there? Now you get to spend that sum on a three-week trip to Fiji!

Ask yourself, would you rather be lounging on a hammock in the middle of the Pacific or hoping to have a car crash in order to get some payback from the black hole that's been siphoning your cash every month for a decade?

Only once did I ever take any form of insurance that wasn't compulsory. That was against car hijacking and theft in South Africa – where ironically enough no form of car insurance was compulsory. And that was because of what I said about Africa: the probabilities of calamity are *actually* quite high. Everybody I knew had had a window smashed in at the very least. That was for two years and I never claimed, but I didn't mind the money because I was in a place where you had to look over your shoulder all the time. Takeaway: if the risks and rewards make sense, go for it by all means. I just think that if you live in a developed country, your risks are probably negligible enough to ignore insurance .

Finally, don't switch off your insurance cynicism just because you're on holiday. Car hire companies get otherwise smart people to hand over millions in extra payments for the ghostly service of 'not sending you a huge bill' when you crash. Well, what kind of a 'service' is that? Why *shouldn't* you get a bill if you break a car? I'd much rather *almost certainly not crash and pay nothing* than *definitely pay something and almost certainly not crash*. To me, the worst-case scenario is about as likely as getting hit by an asteroid. I haven't crashed in 20 years of driving. I'd rather have half that money for a slap-up holiday dinner and put half into my *own* savings account than let some spotty youth take it off my credit card. My way, money piles up that can be used for a thousand different things, just one of which might be a scratched fender in Tenerife. But when you hand over your card, the amount is gone *forever*. Or, if we're pedantic, can only be used in the ultra-specific circumstances of a car accident during a randomly-defined few days of your life.

And then there's travel insurance. If Marco Polo were here today, what do you think he'd say about that? When did we become such fearmongering wimps?

You have to take your hat off to an industry that takes your money and then watches you walk away thinking you've gained something. But once you're finished doing that, how about you resolve not to give them any more of your hard-won cash?

#1 TAKEAWAY Forget the premiums and start putting that money into your own savings account. If it helps, set up a separate one specifically as an 'emergency fund'.

- Monthly total insurance premiums (excluding travel): €20
- Available annual saving: €240
- Bank credit by 40: **€4560**

IMPACT: Squeezing insurance companies means they'll shrink — and so will their office presence. Again, that's less construction and less energy. You'll also be fighting against the culture of fear and the loss of community their products foster.

BONUS TIP: Discuss matters relating to insurance with travel partners before you go. One way or another, discovering a difference of opinion at the car rental counter after a long flight is not going to end well.

BONUS TIP: Neutralise the efforts of the 'life insurance' industry to sow fear on behalf of your loved ones. You can do this by making it very clear to your next of kin that you do *not* want a fancy funeral and *insist* that your remains to be dealt with by the municipality. Then you can all spend the saved insurance money on a party *whilst you're alive to enjoy it*.

---

1. A friend of mine took bicycle cover for several years, only to be refused payout upon its theft because he didn't have documentation to prove that his lock — bought a decade previously! — conformed to some or other quality standard. Such stories abound.

'Other People' and Saving...

Learn to Entertain Yourself

Introverts have a natural advantage over extroverts when it comes to saving.

If you've grasped Dalkey's Law, then you'll agree that reading a book in the garden instead of doing something that costs money is equivalent to *making money*. The problem is that while this is hardly a chore for a bibliophile loner, a lot of people actually can't sit by themselves. They're restless. They don't like their own company. They think something's wrong if they're not out babbling with friends.

And that inevitably leads to more coffee shops, bars and other sundry expenses.

Which category you fall into has a lot to do with your personality — some of us are born, or raised, more gregarious than others. It's way too much to ask the more outgoing folks to stay home alone all the time. (Although the 2020 global lockdown has taught us that we're more capable of it than we thought...) Nonetheless, any of us can at least *try* to find a solo pastime or two that we enjoy as much as going out on the town. Assuming these activities are free or very cheap, then we have far more opportunity to grab a pleasant, painless Dalkey's Law Gig on a regular basis.

That pastime doesn't have to be reading a book — although reading is a *great* example of something most of us loved as kids and somehow dropped as we slipped into frenetic adulthood. We may find, if we make an active effort, that we still adore slipping into a good story as much as we ever did. Taking a moment to rediscover such solo joys opens up a whole new world of savings opportunities for the 'people person'.

I'm the last person to suggest going full hermit is a healthy idea. So don't do that, unless you genuinely thrive on being a recluse. But if you find ways to make doing your own thing pleasure rather than torture, then that's a key weapon for you as a saver. When entertaining yourself is a viable alternative to going out and spending money, you might not always plump for that option. Not every time.

Then, whether you take up gardening, get stuck into cooking or video games, write a novel, build puzzles, learn to play the banjo or simply meditate your way to an appreciation of silence, you'll start to see a difference in your bank account. And since that new hobby is actually *enjoyable*, the corresponding saving is no strain at all!

Perhaps you already found this golden pastime by default during the forced isolation of your local COVID-19 lockdown? And you probably already saw the results reflected in an unusually healthy bank account at the end of the month. (Perhaps, too, in a more balanced outlook and a sense of calm you never had before.) If you liked the look of your savings following those quiet weeks, all you've got to do is keep an element of that life-style going as 'normality' returns!

As you may have noticed, some of the recreation I've mentioned doesn't *have* to be done alone. Partner up with a friend and learn that musical instrument together! Now your 'solo activity' can be sociable after all — and no less cost-effective for that.

If you live with other people or have a family, It ought to be even easier to recruit others to your new free hobbies. It can be companionable, in a refreshing kind of way, to retire to the lawn *with your partner* and each read a book. You don't have to wait for old age to do that! Another alternative? Well, you could even save money by spending more time in the bedroom…

#1 TAKEAWAY Develop at least two 'free' hobbies that you can do on your own. A once-off investment in equipment is okay.

- Monthly saving if you skip one €12 cinema & popcorn outing per week: €48
- Available annual saving: €576
- Bank credit by 40: **€10,944**

IMPACT: Doing something quiet at home is rarely going to be more damaging than whatever entertainment you'd choose outside the house. And you contribute to a quieter, more reflective mood. Something that would hardly go astray anywhere right now…

BONUS TIP: One hack for getting your social fix whilst enjoying the economy of home is simply to invite people over sometimes! It's basic student wisdom: drinking at home is orders of magnitude cheaper than going to bars…

Grow Younger

This world makes it tough to stick to your savings plans. There's temptation at every turn. And unfortunately, your friends, acquaintances and even family can do a great job of playing that devil on your shoulder.

Few savings strategies ever told you to audit the financial impact the people around you are having. But this one does.

When you were a scholar or a student, peer pressure came in different forms. Not many of your mates had their own money. Arguments about splitting restaurant bills were non-existent. Either you didn't go to restaurants at all, because nobody could afford it, or the question of paying a share of somebody else's double bacon burger was abhorred by everyone in equal measure.

As you get older, things start to change. Some of your buddies — even siblings! — may start to earn substantially better than you do. They'll get cars, mortgages, buy bottles of champagne. You may begin to envy elements of their lifestyle and think, 'What am I doing wrong?' That can work as a subtle form of peer pressure. And this variety isn't so dangerous — you can use it as motivation to earn better, save better or both.

But then there's the more explicit kind. People looking around the table and saying, 'We're good to split the bill, right?' People coming up with expensive Airbnb suggestions for the next group holiday. People, like our friend Tom at the airport, assuming you can afford to get in a taxi with them. People buying you expensive presents, which you may then feel pressure to reciprocate.

Both are a normal part of the journey through life.

Don't worry: I'm absolutely not going to suggest that you dump every school buddy the moment they creep above the third tax threshold. Relationships like these are more valuable (and irreplaceable) than anything money can buy. And as for family, well, you're stuck with them!

This book is about how to save *without* making sacrifices of that nature.

There may be some 'relationships', however, that aren't much of a sacrifice at all. Real friends may be non-negotiable, but what about acquaintances? How much do you *really* like some of the people costing you money? Would they come over and help you move furniture? Would they visit you in hospital?

While you answer those questions for your own peer group, you can also keep age in mind as you go forward and make additional friends. There's a lot to be said for surrounding yourself with people a few years your junior for as long as you can get away with it. A 38-year-old who hangs out with 25-year-olds can usually bank on cheaper nights out, activities and holidays than the 35-year-old mixing with folks her own age.

Don't get me wrong: we all need people of our own vintage in our lives. They've journeyed through the same world we have, and that's priceless. But adding a few younger friends to the cocktail is only ever good. It will get you off the sofa more often, give you new, hopeful perspectives to ponder and keep you feeling more spritely than you otherwise might!

#1 TAKEAWAY Make an active effort to hang out with people a few years younger than you are. Mostly appropriate for those in the 25–40 bracket.

- Cost of evening drinking supermarket beer with youngsters: €10
- Cost of food and wine in restaurant with wealthier peers: €25
- Saving if the younger crowd wins out twice per month: €30
- Available annual saving: €360
- Bank credit by 40: **€6840**

IMPACT: While your own generation might be irretrievably stuck in its wasteful ways, younger people are more open to new ideas and keen on changing the world. (Just ask Greta Thunberg!) They're far likelier to take *your* impactful behaviour onboard, not to mention going forth and multiplying it!

BONUS TIP: When evaluating potential new friends — especially those the same age as or older than you — drop hints early on that you follow certain rules with regard to saving money. If they stick around, they're probably not expensive types.

Date With Care

If you're already in a relationship and your financial arrangements are settled, you can probably skip this section. But if
you're single, I'd urge you to read it with great care. This is a
topic that rarely gets a mention in a world that thinks a grinning
Instagram photo together means you're set for life…yet comes
up all too often when divorce is pending.

If you're going to choose a partner at some point in your life,
then you can bet your bottom Dollar (quite literally, in some
cases) that they're going to have a whopping influence on your
ultimate financial situation. Hollywood romance narratives gloss
over this fact. And in the early stages of infatuation, so do we.

Try not to let fresh love blind you to realities that could impact
your future bank balance. I'm not just talking dangers and
pitfalls here — the signs may also be positive ones. It might not
be that your future spouse looks likely to use your credit card
irresponsibly: they might be the one helping *you* save better. And
it's not just an opposing personality that can affect you one way
or the other: a romantic interest with a similar outlook can also
be an enabler for existing habits.

If you're dating with a view to anything longer-term, you want to seek out a clear, early impression of your partner's approach to saving. If you need to get better at saving — and I assume you do if you're reading this — then recognise that dating someone frugal might be good for you. This means making an active decision that their role is a positive influence. Otherwise, you'll be fighting about money before you know it.

Equally, be aware that getting involved with a careless spender, someone with expensive tastes or no interest in sustainability has the potential to undo all the good habits you're reading about right now. So make sure you test them on this stuff right upfront — and don't let Cupid mess with the plan! A first date in an expensive restaurant can set a dangerous level of expectation. It's far better to start with a free walk or similar for your initial meetup, and make sure to drop at least one hint that you like the fact it's free. If your date runs away at the mention of sound financial policy, they're obviously not compatible with your outlook. If they don't, then great! Fancier treats can come later — when they will be understood as such.

Before you completely dismiss someone as a money drain, however, do find out if they give much thought to planet Earth! If you at least share similar views on sustainability, then there's hope! As I said at the beginning, some people find thinking about saving money *per se* difficult, but are more than keen to think about positive and impactful behaviour. They may not see the link between the two. But as long as that link exists, then a potential fight about money strategy can just as easily be reframed as a positive decision to live more responsibly!

#1 TAKEAWAY Ask yourself the difficult questions about a potential partner's relationship with money. Do this analysis away from them and any emotional influences.

- Monthly cost if your partner adds €100 to your outgoings: €100
- Annual saving if you have a 'cheaper' partner: €1200
- Bank credit by 40: **€22,800**

IMPACT: Getting dragged into bad habits by your future partner means Earth just lost one person who was hitherto willing to make an effort! You wanna be that guy?

BONUS TIP: The first time you get the chance to see your new interest's home, open your eyes to the stuff on display. Do you see over-the-top electronics or ornaments? How many brand names are lying around? Do they have a penchant for disposable stuff? Your first visit will reveal most of what you need to know about both their spending and sustainability habits.

Go Childless

Having children is, by all accounts, *wildly* expensive. And since each person we add to the global population is another mouth to feed for a lifetime, they can never hope to compete with a nonexistent person for sustainability cred.

If you're weighing up building a family, and you decide against it, then congratulations: you just saved by far the biggest number you'll see anywhere in the book! Meanwhile, a little slice of Amazon rainforest, spared from being cleared for crops to feed animals to feed people, will send you a thank you card.

How much is *wildly* expensive, exactly? Well, there's no catch-all answer to such a complex and variable calculation. But plenty have studied the costs in far greater depth than I have. The Child Poverty Action Group is just one of them. In their Cost of a Child Report 2020, they concluded that the full cost up to the age of 18 in the United Kingdom is a whopping £152,747. (€177,000 at the time of writing.) And that's just the calculation for a couple — lone parents can expect it to cost them £185,413 (€215,000 as I write).

And that's before you think about having a second and a third…

Worth noting: the numbers above will buy you your own (modest) home in most parts of the world. Even in a capital city. In cash. Outright.

This is a topic that makes people emotional. For existing parents, certain reactions are understandable. Having committed to the biggest time and money outlay of their lives, and one from which there's no turning back, the only coping mechanism is to aggressively defend that decision the moment it's questioned.

Which is a roundabout way of saying there's no sense in my going any deeper in this section. I've stated some thought-provoking facts and won't be labouring the point any further.

#1 TAKEAWAY Don't have kids. Or at least have fewer.

- Saving per child you don't have (per person, in couple scenario, rounded down): €88,500
- Bank credit at 40[1]: €88,500

IMPACT: The entire impact one human has on this planet over a lifetime! Thanks to you, that impact isn't happening.

BONUS TIP: If you absolutely must have a small person biting your ankles, why not adopt one? There are plenty of kids in the world in need of parents…

BONUS TIP: If you do go down the kids route, at least resist the urge to shower them with plastic toys at Christmas. The rate at which this stuff gets forgotten and binned is criminal. Come up with creative, low-impact alternatives that will teach your child not to go through life as a careless consumer.

_____

1. I know a lot of people are well past 40 by the time their kids are 18, but I'll keep things consistent here. As throughout this book, the bank balance is the one that really matters!

Eating and Drinking

Peanut Butter Sandwiches (aka the hidden perils of weekday lunches)

When I first started working, in London, it took less than four hours in my new job for me to become acquainted with the odd habit of 'running to Tesco to pick up a sandwich' at lunchtime.

I toddled along with my colleagues, curious to see what this strange custom was all about. *My* plan was to buy an entire loaf of bread and enough peanut butter to last me a couple of weeks. *Their* plan, it turned out, was to pay at least as much — if not more — for a single sandwich, lovingly put together in the small hours by some robot in Derbyshire.

Funny thing is, the weirdo in that story was apparently *me*!

Looking at the €5472 extra I've got in the bank 20 years later (yes, really! See the calculation below...), and considering that my self-made, personalised sandwiches were just as good as any of theirs and only took 10 minutes to make, I'd say being the weirdo really paid. Every time I made a sandwich it was a tiny Dalkey's Law Gig. And those daily gigs added up to a stellar payout.

Do we really think that just because we reach a point where we're no longer school kids and begin to earn money, bringing a brightly coloured, rectangular lunchbox for our midday meal is beneath us? That we now ought to pay someone else for a mass-produced sandwich? Anybody, no matter how incompetent they are in the kitchen, can throw two bits of bread together. If, like me, you're not organised enough to do it before work, you can do your slicing and spreading in the office kitchen. But I really hope you're not paying over the odds, every day of your working life, for some machine to slap two pieces of rye either side of a lettuce leaf and a slice of Emmental…

Going to the pub for lunch is a different story. You're treating yourself to a hot meal prepared by someone with access to proper cooking equipment, which you don't have right now. If it's a local independent, you're supporting your community too. And you're likely spending some quality time with your work-mates. I have no issue with any of this. But heavens above, how it pains me to see people do supermarket sandwiches! Because they're a savings-eater you can kill with nothing more than a tiny modicum of effort and creativity.

The broader point is this: weekday work lunches have a pernicious effect on most people's savings. And yet, played right, they can do precisely the opposite. That's because most of us do work lunchtimes five days a week, roughly 48 weeks a year. The consequences of our spending habits (whether good or bad) concerning work lunches multiply fast.

And it's all too easy to fall into habits and favourites when we keep dashing out to grab something in the same small (and expensive, if we work in fashionable city centres) radius around our workplace. But these routines are among the first we should look to break if we want to improve our savings record.

Doing so doesn't necessarily have to be much of a challenge. When we pop out to grab 'our usual', we're acting from force of habit. It's not like we're even all that passionate about the thing we're buying: when did a Pickle & Cheddar from the super-market ever get the pulse racing?

That's why it makes such sense to cut out damaging dependen-cies when you're on the run at lunchtime, and rather save your money for moments where you can really enjoy your food.

What change can *you* make? It doesn't matter whether you move from industrial sandwiches to your own creations, or from the €10 pub main course to the €7 lunch special: even a tiny adjust-ment will have an astounding effect over the weeks, months and years...

#1 TAKEAWAY Don't follow the herd at lunch hour. Bringing your own sandwich (or similar) is worth thousands over the course of a career.

- Cost of supermarket sandwich: €2
- Cost of loaf of bread & jar of peanut butter (or alternative condiment) for the week: €4
- Weekly gain on the sandwich-buyers: €6
- Monthly saving from making own sandwiches: €24
- Available annual saving: €288
- Bank credit by 40: **€5472**

IMPACT: Your 'lazy sandwich' made in some horrible depot is an unnecessary addition to the carbon-belching logistics machine. You're sparing the planet this, as well as the awful plastic in which it's usually sealed.

BONUS TIP: Bringing dinner leftovers works just as well as bringing a sandwich. It's not as cheap, but still probably cheaper than what your colleagues will pick up! It's a nice way to mix things up, too!

Stop Succumbing (aka patience pays)

Here's where I tell you to think twice about ducking into a store and grabbing a bottle of Coke, just because you're on the move and you're thirsty.

I'm not talking about actual meals here. Nor occasional hankerings, like when you crave something sweet. Sometimes I can't stop myself grabbing bottles of chocolate milk after lunch on a warm day either! As long as these moments aren't a compulsive habit, then your wallet's staying in shape and so are you. I'm talking about automatically heeding your body's call for a hit of food or drink the moment you hear it.

We live in a world of *now*. Everything has to happen right this second, or we think something's gone awfully wrong. Given the on-demand availability of nearly anything, it's no wonder we confuse instant gratification with genuine need. So when we feel mildly thirsty, and we're nowhere near a tap, we automatically think, 'Where can I get a drink *now*?' as opposed to 'I'll need a drink sometime soonish.' Then, before we know it, another Euro (bottled water) or three (raspberry-ginger-carrot-kale shake) are gone forever. Unlike the bottle, of course: the planet may have to deal with *that* for millennia.

I'm not encouraging you to die of thirst or starvation. If you're on the doorstep of the last shop before you wander into the Mojave, I want you to get your butt in there and stock up on every provision your little arms can carry. But most of us aren't staggering around on the fringes of a desert, are we? Most of us are pottering about in cities, and we're going to be at some kind of free/cheaper water or snack source real soon: the office, the apartment or perhaps just a decent restroom. Humans can go three days without water and three weeks without food, which I think puts a half an hour's patience into perspective. So when I'm a little peckish or could use a drink, I always ask myself: 'Can't I hang on just a while? Do I really *need* this *now*? Or am I just being a spoilt little kid?'

Saying 'no' to a few of these in-between food and drink purchases will add up to savings of at least four figures by the time most of us are 40. And if the money doesn't convince you to show a little patience now and then, here are a couple of compelling social reasons to hold your horses when it makes sense to do so.

First, every bottled drink you buy is more than likely a plastic one that will take about a zillion years to decompose in the ocean, if at all. The only bottles that belong in the sea are bottlenose dolphins. All of whom will thank you kindly for waiting to get to a tap.

Second, if you're with other people and use the dolphin thing as an explanation for why you're not buying anything, you're likely to be judged favourably. You'll probably sow a seed in their thinking, which might change their decision the next time. Look, the dolphins love you even more now!

Third, so much of the 'on-the-run' food and drink on offer is junk that will make you fat and perhaps die young. Want to be a poor lump of lard with a low life expectancy, or healthier and richer for longer? The choice is yours…

#1 TAKEAWAY If running into stores between meals is a regular habit for you, try to wean yourself off it. You could start by limiting yourself to doing it 1–2 times a week. Ask a friend or colleague to keep score and hold you to account.

- Total cost of three 'impatient' food/drink purchases per week: €6
- Monthly potential saving: €24
- Available annual saving: €288
- Bank credit by 40: **€5472**

IMPACT: If we all consume fewer drinks and snacks, then fewer will be manufactured and shipped. This saves energy, packaging and emissions.

Question Your Food

Food is a tricky topic for anyone trying to save money *and* the planet in one fell swoop. There's a bit of a conflict. Because the organic, free-range, ethical stuff's always more expensive, isn't it? Sometimes it can feel like truly guilt-free shopping is a privilege for the wealthy.

I haven't got an easy solution to this one. It is absolutely right and logical that responsibly produced food should cost more. Factory farming and its brethren became the norm because its economies of scale made production cheaper and thus more profitable. We've all supported its rise. Now, if we want a world without some of the horrific 'agricultural' scenes that will put you off your dinner for a week, we have to be prepared to pay more for our food. And if we live in a country with expensive land, high living standards and lots of regulation, we can't necessarily expect our food to be local *and* cheap.

This is one reason why I believe our weekly grocery shop is the last place we should compromise in a bid to save cash. And there's another good reason to spend a bit more: your own health. I'm no expert here, but nobody seems to think that living off processed foods is good for you — and processed food is most commonly the cheap stuff. You want to live long and enjoy all the money you've saved, right? So don't put *too* much thought into saving on dinner ingredients.

Right then, so we're going to pick the more sustainable options from the shelves insofar as we can afford to take the hit. If you still need motivating, remind yourself that they do tend to taste better! In fact, when you think about it like that, I'd argue that being able to afford all of the tastiest and most 'responsible' food is one of the rewards we get for saving on ultra-mundane stuff like phone contracts.

Besides, there are other ways we can reduce our grocery bill.

I'm not referring to customer rewards cards. I don't even bother with them. For one thing, they keep you coming back to the same store when it might be cheaper to shop around — that's a false economy. And you'll never get around to supporting your local deli or farmer's market if you've always got a raft of 'expiring soon' vouchers to use at the supermarket. Big business knows what it's doing!

One positive, cost-efficient thing you can always do is prioritise items discounted due to an impending sell-by date. Chucking these in the trolley isn't just a bargain, it's the right thing to do! Help banish food waste by coming into the store with an open mind rather than an inflexible shopping list. You never know what you're going to get, so be prepared to throw something eclectic together — that can be a lot of fun in itself! If it's meat, you can also just throw it in the freezer for another time.

You can also save sustainably (and substantially!) just by taking your diet in a more vegetarian direction. Like most South Africans, I adore all manner of meats (ideally cooked over an open fire), but I have to consider that our dependent attachment to dead animals is causing this planet some serious issues. It's hard for me to cut back on steak and lamb chops, but the (rightly) growing price of these carnivorous options pushes me to make veggie choices more often. Just another example of how both kinds of saving work together!

Lastly, where can you cut out the shopping altogether? Are there a few vegetables you could grow yourself? If space is limited, then choose a plant that keeps on giving — Swiss chard, for example. Could you learn how to fish the occasional meal out of a nearby river or the sea? Are you willing to go hunting for a spot of venison? The supplies scare that came with COVID-19 brought these basic survival practices back into fashion, but food security's not the only reason to give them a close look.

Any step towards some control over your own food supply is likely to save you money (even considering fishing/hunting licence fees and equipment) if you do it regularly. Sure, given the time commitments and relatively slow returns here, it probably *does* make more sense to earn money some other way and buy your food from the shops. In pure Dalkey's Law terms, you probably don't have reason enough to grow your own carrots.

But you're not reading this book with *only* financial efficiency in mind, are you? What food could be more clean, local and emission-free than that which you just shot in the woods, hooked out of the river or harvested from a pot on your balcony? And hey, your new hobby's getting you fresh air and exercise too!

#1 TAKEAWAY Eat vegetarian (fresh, local ingredients only) at least 3–4 days per week.

- Cost of two juicy chicken breasts: €6
- Monthly saving if you abstain from adding one to your weekly stir-fry: €12
- Available annual saving: €144
- Bank credit by 40: **€2736**

IMPACT: Every food purchasing decision we make is the last link in a chain that can stretch back as far as a felled tree in South America or a strangled dolphin in the Pacific.[1]

BONUS TIP: Find out which days are best for picking up discounted food at your local store. The night before a shop closure, be it for a weekend or public holiday, often sees a frenzy of red or yellow stickers going on stock that needs to be cleared. Also, save even more money and waste with apps like Too Good To Go.

---

1. The 'Logistics' chapter in *The Pleasures and Sorrows of Work* by Alain de Botton is a must-read if you're struggling to picture the enormity of that chain.

Rethink Restaurants

I told you this book wasn't about all-consuming deprivation. Which is why I'm all for you going to a nice restaurant for dinner now and then. This is usually going to cost more than eating at home. Doing it all the time isn't part of a good savings plan. But once or twice a week — why not? It's often a good opportunity to support a local business or food supplier. And if you make smart decisions when you're there, you can make it sustainable for your wallet too.

Some things are obvious, but I'll mention them anyway. Take your own bottle of wine if that's an option — or choose a restaurant where it is. Order a jug of tap water (see 'Trust Your Tap') so you don't quench your thirst by glugging the expensive stuff down. If you're on holiday in a foreign language, learn *how* to order tap water rather than something in a (probably plastic) bottle with bubbles. I won't go through the global lexicon here, but I've found that *carafe d'eau* and *Leitungswasser* do the job in French and German respectively.

Even more obviously, look at the prices on the menu — unless someone else (preferably someone rich) has promised to pay!

Unless it's your 50th wedding anniversary, you should automatically rule out the more expensive items. Keeping it under €15 for a main course is a rule of thumb I've always followed. If there are no main courses under that price, then I'm afraid you haven't picked a savings-friendly restaurant. And you're probably going to need *two* main courses because the portions will be tiny!

If you have a menacingly large appetite such as mine, a buffet will often deliver superb value for money. Particularly if it's breakfast or lunch, where you might be able to stuff yourself so full that you don't need the next meal at all.

I suffer from a sugary tooth as much as I do from gluttonous tendencies, and I'm no stranger to the temptations of the dessert menu. So I'm not going to tell you to skip your treacle tart. But I *am* going to suggest you share it.

Dessert prices, in proportion to the amount you get, are often inflated. Also consider that unlike the main course, which has to fill you up, the *quantity* of dessert you'll eat isn't all that important. If they give you a whopping portion, you'll eat it, but it's actually more about a) the anticipation of its arrival and b) getting a taste. Neither of which you have to give up if you ask for two forks and share a portion, right?

Sharing will knock two or three Euros off your bill, be kind to your waistline and — if you're on a promising date — add a desirable level of intimacy to proceedings. Triple win! If you're *not* on a date, try to share with someone who likes to show off how much money they have. They'll probably wave away your contribution come bill time. (By the way, waving away contributions isn't a good saving strategy for *you*.)

The thorny topic of how to split bills in a group gets a lot of people hot under the collar, and with good reason. If you're going to dinner with people who think it's okay to make you pay for the steak and champagne they ordered, without at least clearing it first, then it's time for a good look at the folk you're hanging out with (see also 'Grow Younger'). Because real friends wouldn't be that thoughtless unless they're used to throwing huge sums of money around — in which case, they can pay the whole damn bill, can't they?

Then there's tipping. Like all small outlays, tips will really add up over time. It can feel nice to tip, sure. Do it by all means, if the service was good and you think the waitress looks like the proverbial exploited student. Equally, if it's a small family place and the 'waitress' is also the owner, then why are you tipping someone who personally set a price they consider fair? And don't be guilted into it after the waiter brought you a burger with a tomato on it after you *specifically* asked them to hold the salad.

Tipping gets trickier when you're on holiday and don't know the culture. There are places where they might chase you down the road if you fail to leave something extra[1], but there are *also* places where they don't have a clue what to do with a tip. It's frequently the case in Asia, for example. Check what the local customs are before you give people money they're not expecting or may even find offensive.

#1 TAKEAWAY When you're choosing meals in a restaurant, lay a serviette over all the main courses over €15. Now they're off your menu!

- Saving if you buy €15 main course instead of €20 main course, visiting a restaurant once a week: €5
- Available annual saving: €260
- Bank credit by 40: **€4940**

IMPACT: Going for lower prices usually means sidestepping imported foods, fish and meat. All of which contributes to a more sustainable world. This isn't a hard-and-fast rule, though, so don't judge your impact by price alone!

BONUS TIP: Torn between dessert and coffee? Take the latter and mix in a generous heap of sugar. Now you have both for the price of one!

BONUS TIP: Some restaurants will try to guilt you into buying their bottled water, to the point of pretending they misunderstood your order. One way to handle this is to explain that it's about the pollution, not the money. I've heard of waiters becoming *very* apologetic when people take this approach. You're also likely to inspire everyone within earshot to think about the bigger picture, which is a good thing.

---

1. Tel Aviv, since you ask…

Trust Your Tap

Let's get one thing straight, once and for all. Unless you're living or travelling in a developing country (and no, that doesn't mean Spain, my north European friends), tap water *will not kill you*.

We humans have been drinking out of muddy ponds for most of our history. Every other animal still does. So can we stop bigging ourselves up with the ridiculous notion that nothing but Evian will do? It's *more* than enough that we have clean, treated water running 24/7 from various orifices in our homes. The more we mollycoddle our stomachs, the more sensitive we're going to get, and the more ridiculous the cycle becomes. So let's *stop* it.

Water out of bottles is unnecessary pollutant number one on this planet. According to *National Geographic*[1], a million plastic beverage bottles are sold *every minute*. Where do we think they all go? Environmental catastrophes aside, there's the damage it does to your finances to consider. Even if you're only a one-a-day kind of person, the numbers might make you feel faint when you see them below.

Yes, there are places (Africa, India) where you ought to run a mile from the tap water if you're not used to it.[2] But for all those weeks in the year when you're not making an ashram pilgrimage, are you really telling me you need to spend money on something you've already paid for with your water bill?

#1 TAKEAWAY If you live in a developed country, take a simple vow never to buy bottled water again. Unless you're donating it to some place that actually depends on the stuff for survival.

- Cost of daily bottle of water: €1
- Available annual saving: €365
- Bank credit by 40: **€6935**

IMPACT: Just search the internet for pictures of 'plastic bottle beach'. Do you want things to look like that when you string up your hammock in Fiji one day? This is real, folks. But changing our behaviour is the easiest way to turn the problem around.

BONUS TIP: Make a habit of carrying a water bottle you fill up at home and any time you pass a tap. Especially in summer. Instant gratification on the run — but free.

BONUS TIP: While water is the easiest bottled liquid to cut out, consider the packaging when you buy other drinks too. Is there a glass or metal alternative, perhaps? And don't forget that watering-down is an option for juice-type beverages: one bottle of concentrate can replace several bottles of pre-mix.

---

1. *National Geographic*, September 2021 issue.
2. For more details, dive into the World Health Organisation/UNICEF data at https://washdata.org/data/household/

Consider That Coffee!

I won't bang on about coffee, because every book with even a passing interest in saving is going to tell you to cut the cappuccinos. But there's a good reason they all say it, so it would be remiss of me not to mention the black stuff too.

Sitting down and enjoying a €3,50 barista coffee as an experiential treat? Absolutely fine.

Coffee at home? You have my blessing.

Coffee from that dodgy machine at the office? No problem. The taste will grow on you.

Making that daily latte-on-the-run a *must*? You're killing your financial future to the tune of almost €25,000. Nobody *must* have coffee. That's an addiction-feeding myth. The stuff didn't even get to Europe until the late 16th century. Frothy, expensive barista varieties are a way more recent invention glorified by hipsters, go-getters and *Frasier*. They're nothing other than a luxury. A €3,50 drink has no place on the daily diet of people earning average salaries.

#1 TAKEAWAY Start by reducing that latte-on-the run to alternate days. Then twice a week. Then just Fridays. Continue until you reach the point where you can 'take it or leave it'.

- Cost of daily cappuccino: €3.50
- Available annual saving: €1277.50
- Bank credit by 40: **€24,272.50**

IMPACT: Even if you've embraced re-usable cups (and you should!), cutting out the steamed stuff will still contribute to reducing demand for dairy or soy products.[1] As for the coffee itself, there's a lot of water usage tied up with its production — and unless you live in Colombia or Kenya, it has a horrific carbon footprint too.

BONUS TIP: If you want a compromise, drink *espresso*. It's half the price. It doesn't involve cows and their greenhouse gases! And you can get a fine home machine with your first month or two of latte savings…

BONUS TIP: A flask is a great investment if you want to make a decent coffee at home and enjoy it on the run. Do you need to buy a brand-new one, though? Read the next chapter before you decide!

---

1. Have you seen how many bottles of milk (often plastic…) a busy coffee shop goes through in an hour?

Things and Stuff

Boycott IKEA

Before IKEA's lawyers come for me, let me say that the title of this chapter is actually a back-handed compliment. The Swedish company has achieved the ultimate blend of brand power, attractive pricing and reliable convenience. They've done it so well that 'the IKEA trip' has become an undisputed rite of passage for anyone moving into a new home. Something only weirdos and outliers would dare to question. That's why I had to plump for it as a synonym for the unthinking purchase of new stuff.

Now here's the thing: if you're keen on saving money, the planet or both, then it's time to be an outlier and a weirdo. It's time to look past the clever store layouts, the shiny catalogues and the 3D home décor app on your tablet. It's time to take heed of an uncomfortable fact that IKEA and other purveyors of brand-new non-consumables don't want you to know.

A fact that no amount of sustainable, local manufacturing will cancel out.

That fact? *There is enough of everything already.*

I'm not sure how to prove what I'm about to say, but I'm going to go out on a limb here and state that if the world stopped producing ironing boards for the next 50 years, we'd be fine. The same goes for sofas, beds, chairs, tables, desks, lamps, plates, brooms, extension leads and bookshelves. Take one look at your local online used-goods marketplace and you'll get a hint of what I mean: people are *giving* this stuff away.

Isn't that disgusting?

We've been the victims of gentle 'aspiration massage' by marketing people (and our peers) for so long that we actually think it's okay to turn our noses up at perfectly functional stuff that's free — or damn near to it. To wave that hand-me-down coffee table away and say, 'Have it sent to the landfill!' To ball our fists like stroppy kids and say, 'But I don't *want* grandma's ugly old mugs!' All because we want our living rooms and kitchens to look like some identikit postcard of middle-class bliss.

It makes my stomach turn.

Our great-grandchildren will curse us for this hubris.

We do *not* need new household stuff!

It all looks the same, anyway. Who decided every apartment in the western world had to be a sad blend of grey, white and beige? These are colours that scream mediocrity at you all day long. In a world that's supposed to be all about personalisation, why do we adhere to some pastel catalogue standard for our homes? Do we think alpaca wool and bright orange walls are only for hippies?

Getting on your local equivalent of Craigslist is like a lucky-dip wonderland. Not only will you spend less money — possibly none! — but you'll end up with a unique, individual, colourful home that radiates wonder and frivolity. And which tells of an owner who knows their place in the world.

Even struggling young couples accept 'the IKEA trip' because it's essentially a one-off. And with that in mind, the prices always seem reasonable. It's true that the savings involved in furnishing your apartment second-hand might be as little as a couple of hundred Euros. And since it's not a recurring economy, I've skipped doing a calculation below.

But just because we can afford something, does that make it right that we have it?

#1 TAKEAWAY Make 'buying new' the exception rather than the rule. Unless you're purchasing underwear (there are a few things nobody wants to inherit!), make your local second-hand marketplaces your default first port of call.

IMPACT: You're helping bring the production of unnecessary goods (and their mindless packaging) to a standstill. Your choices with regard to home furnishings and appliances also leave a powerful, yet humble, visual impression on your visitors. And that might, in turn, inspire them to rethink their choices too.

BONUS TIP: If you're struggling with the mindset change I'm talking about, take a trip to a really poor country. Hang out in some *barrios*. Meet families living in a single room. By the time you get home, you'll have a different view on the importance of matching cushions.

Be a Share-Bear

How often do use your vacuum cleaner?

When you stop and think about it, doesn't the idea of every apartment in a building owning a machine they might only use once a fortnight strike you as just a little bit insane? It's almost the perfect caricature of wastefulness.

Surrounded by an all-consuming culture of individualism, we've been sucked into (!) thinking that this kind of behaviour is normal and justifiable.

My hope is that COVID-19 has brought that oversight into extremely sharp focus going forward.

Sustainability aside, sharing vacuum cleaners with your neighbours has always made sense from a savings perspective too. I don't think you need me to go into the mechanics of how pool-purchasing a machine like that makes it cheaper for everyone.

The trouble is that people think you're a weirdo for suggesting it. 'I can afford my own, thanks very much!' they would harrumph, failing completely to see that this isn't the point. That it's not about showing how financially independent we are.

But the pandemic has put things in perspective. We have a window — possibly a very brief one, considering the phenomenon of collective amnesia — during which it might be acceptable to propose a vacuum-sharing scheme in your building. With the stark lessons of COVID-19 as your secret weapon, you don't even need to sell people on the savings thing. They're far more likely to be receptive to the critical need for responsible consumption.

The point here isn't to get into the nuts and bolts of sharing vacuum cleaners with neighbours. That's just one small, easy way we could 'save money and save the planet' with a slight change in attitude. My message is that we open our eyes to opportunities to share resources where it makes sense to do so. Whether it's the use of a car, an elusive Allen key or the proverbial spoonful of sugar, we need to start waking up to the possibility of more communal thinking.

Our current ways are little more than the product of habit. When we need something for occasional use, we rush out and buy our own. Or perhaps we think, 'That's too expensive, so I'll have to go without.' There's a middle ground, folks! Let's start asking ourselves if the guy next door has that thing already. Or wants to go halves on one.

More often than not, the reason we're reluctant with this stuff is we worry people will think we're being cheap. The product of us living in a time of plenty, this thought pattern has become a dangerously destructive one for us all. It's time we grew out of it. Let's not be shy to say what I just said above: sharing is a win on multiple fronts. In a post-pandemic world that has rediscovered the notion of scarce resources by witnessing empty store shelves (however briefly) for the first time since the 1940s, you may find a more sympathetic audience than you would pre-2020.

And remember: a 'neighbour' could be anywhere in the world. When we're done with that device we bought off Amazon for a single job, why don't we ask our social network if anyone else needs the same thing? If it was cheap, we could give it away. If it was expensive, they could give us half the money we paid and we could send it to them by post. Everyone concerned saves money, while the world is spared a perfectly good item being remanufactured for no good reason.

That's an illustration that 'sharing' needn't literally mean there's no money involved. We can also *rent* items to each other — and that goes way further than Airbnb or Turo. Taking the time to sell something second-hand is just a variation on the idea that sharing can reduce our costs (in this case by getting some of our money back) and help the environment (by preventing more new stuff being made). Taking the time to *buy* something second-hand achieves the same ends. Doing either is a neat little Dalkey's Law Gig. And both — or even giving unwanted stuff away online — help to sustain a well-stocked marketplace people can count on.

Which brings me to the point that we have, in the internet, an excellent tool for matching our resource needs. This we all know, but I want to underline that we're only just beginning to use it for that purpose. Keep an eye out for platforms enabling the broad notion of sharing, both on a local and global basis. This is an area likely to get considerable attention in the period following COVID-19. And you, both as a smart saver and responsible citizen, have a duty to support such initiatives.

Just one example of a place you could start is <u>Fat Llama</u>, a platform for renting some of the items most people would rather buy. Make sure to have a good look around <u>Shareable</u> too!

Sure, sharing can sometimes take a little more time and effort than some of the easier options available (1-click shopping for new stuff, anyone?). Maybe we don't always have instant access to something. But now that Dalkey's Law is our guiding principle, we know that spending zero (or a reduced amount) has real financial outcomes. Which means, of course, that we can almost always put a price on the time we spend, the trouble we take or the patience we show. Not to mention our positive environmental impact, the feel-good factor and the community spirit we'll build.

#1 TAKEAWAY Before you think 'where can I buy X', first think 'who might want to share/lend me X'.

- Monthly fixed car costs (insurance, maintenance, licensing, tax, depreciation): €120
- Available annual saving if you cut costs 50% by sharing with a neighbour: €720
- Bank credit by 40: **€13,680**

IMPACT: Every time you share something, rather than buy another one, you're helping cut both manufacturing and the consequent waste. The sky really is the limit here.

BONUS TIP: Show that you're *not* just out for your own gain by making the first move. Post a notice (think online, too) listing the things you're willing to share or club together on. Be the one to inspire. It'll come back to you.

Make Things Last

If you take a given consumable that lasts for a year, then you're going to need about 80 of them over a lifetime. Make that same thing last for *two* years, of course, and now you'll only need 40.

Hardly ground-breaking mathematics, I know. You would think we all have an innate understanding of this. But when you consider the 'bin it' culture that surrounds us, I'm not so sure that's the case.

The savings here are usually straightforward Dalkey's Law Gigs. Take a little time to maintain or repair something, and you'll be rewarded by having to buy it less often. Ergo, you saved money. Sure, an exact calculation is tough, thanks to the impossible 'less often for how long?' question. Nor does it help that the effects can be very slow. A lot of people find it hard to appreciate that re-covering their mildly unsightly sofa in 2020, so that it gets a stay of execution until 2027, will have *lasting consequence*. Even if they never do such a smart thing again, they'll always be one sofa ahead of the game. Which could mean, when they're pensioners, that what they've got at that point could last them through to the end of their days.

And who wouldn't want to strike 'buy sofa' from the expenses list (not to mention the to-do list!) in their dotage?

As ever, it's not just about saving money. It's about saving land-fills, too. It could even be about leaving something for the kids — or future generations in general. (See also 'Boycott IKEA')

We're not just talking items as big as couches. Even aluminium foil is an opportunity to stretch a lifespan. If the piece covering your take-out isn't too gross, why not fold it up and use it again? Yeah, the financial savings here are minimal. But training such habits will help you spot more substantial gains when they're on offer. And anyway, helping cut waste should be its own reward.

At the risk of stating the obvious, making things last longer often means repairing them. Yet we lack the fix-it mentality of previous generations. Admittedly, a large part of that is the fault of an unethical global manufacturing corps serving its own interests. For example, nobody without the right software can do much under the hood of a car these days. And when plastic things snap, there's no screwing them back together like you could in the wood era. Meanwhile, built-in redundancy on elec-tronics has encouraged us laypeople to declare that it's 'easier to get a new one' the moment things get tough. These money-making tactics are not our fault.

But there are things we can do. First, let's make more careful assessments about whether it really *is* impossible to repair some-thing. Are we just being lazy? Ask around. Get on YouTube. Speak to a geeky friend. Try a factory reset. Borrow tools from a neighbour if you need to. (See also 'Be a Share-Bear') Remem-ber, Dalkey's Law could very well pay you for your time.

We can also support manufacturers of longer-lasting things by buying quality (preferably guaranteed) stuff in the first place. If you purchase a cheap suitcase that only lasts five years, you'll have to buy it three times in the 15 years an expensive one might last you. But even if the cost of both strategies over 15 years is the same, one is clearly less wasteful and shipping-intensive than the other. I did it the first way for many years, which was fine for my savings, but I've come to learn that this was wrong: there's a far more responsible way to reach the same bank balance.

We can even contribute (and save!) as second owners. For example, there are reputable companies refurbishing computers. They do proper paperwork and even offer serious guarantees. I'm typing this on a refurbished iMac that's seven years old, which I bought from AfB in Vienna. It cost under €400 and does the same stuff a new, four-figure one does. Like with the cheap suitcase, it's unlikely to last as long, but at least I'm giving myself a chance to get lucky on that. And even if I *do* need three refurbs in the timespan one new machine would last, spending similar money overall, I'm helping to keep a culture of repair alive. And when we support fixer-uppers to make a living — as opposed to funding holidays for Apple shareholders — we'll still have people who know how to make our own broken goods work again. It's a virtuous cycle.

Finally, even if that footstool, pillow or garden hoe is *genuinely* no longer fit for purpose, make sure to read the next section before you head for the dump!

#1 TAKEAWAY What can you do today to stop something being unnecessarily thrown out? Watch everything from the quality of goods you buy to the sell-by dates in your kitchen.

- Price of a new mobile phone (conservative): €400
- Number of new phones you *don't* have to buy over 19 years if you can make your phone last three years instead of two: Three[1]
- Bank credit by 40: **€1200**

IMPACT: Less electronic waste, less food waste, less general waste. You're also ensuring less new stuff is being churned out, shipped, then dumped in 2030.

---

1. The formula I've used is 19/2 minus 19/3, giving an exact number of 3.16. Like all things in this book, I've stayed on the conservative side in my rounding-off!

Upcycle

What's 100% cheaper than buying something? Making it from things you already have!

And what's more sustainable than throwing something into the sea? Turning it into something useful, of course!

I could hardly leave such a blatant win-win out of a book like this, could I?

Beyond the raw thrift and ecological benefits of repurposing the innumerable random items we accumulate, get set for an almost preposterous jolt of satisfaction every time you come up with another upcycling solution. It stems, I think, from the fact that chances to combine practicality and creativity are so rare in modern life. Turning a broken sock drawer on its side and calling it a book-shelf is like doing art — but a more useful strain of it than you'll find at the Tate Modern. Necessity can also be the mother of inspiration.

Upcycling is an absolute kick — and I say that as someone utterly inept when it comes to making things from scratch. I failed school woodwork projects where all you had to do was glue two blocks together. I hammer nails through my fingers. I drill holes and worry about their positions later. So don't flip the page just because you're not a handyman who hangs out in hardware stores. This is different.

What a pleasant section this is to write! Because there are barely any counter-arguments I need to tackle. Why *wouldn't* you upcycle? It's actually *more* effort to go to the store (or sometimes even Google) and buy the appropriate item. The only thing that puts people off, I think, is that they're worried about colour and style clashes. Maybe that's true by some measures. But by others, it counts as cool. Upcycling is hipster.

Just a few solutions I've got around my house include: coffee jars as pen holders, broken sock drawers as bookshelves, freezer drawers as sock drawers, pallets as bed frames and coffee tables, foosball tables as bathroom cabinets, chairs as DVD player stands, butter containers as soap dishes, pots with destroyed nonstick as herb gardens, dictionaries as iMac height adjusters, beer crates as bedside tables and a punctured air mattress as insulation for my sound studio. I even managed to make my own COVID-19 mask out of an old bag and some string! And that's for a guy with no skill whatsoever. *You* can probably do much better.

Remember, things don't have to be broken to be repurposed. There was nothing wrong with my freezer drawer, for example, but my sock drawer *had* just broken when I was struggling to fit everything into the freezer and realised that having a drawer there was only limiting me. All I had to do was make a connection between these two facts.

There's no need to restrict your raw materials to things you find at home. Whether you look online, venture to the dump or even raid supermarket loading bays (where do you think I got the pallets?), there are a hundred and one free, sustainable ways to deal with your latest household need.

The amount of money you save by upcycling is impossible for me to quantify in any meaningful way. It depends, of course, on what you're rescuing and how often. But even if it's minimal, there's nothing like the rush of knowing you've made a creative and probably unique contribution to reducing waste!

#1 TAKEAWAY Imagine it's the mother of all lockdowns: shops are closed, there's no internet and rubbish collection is on hold. Then watch your creative repurposing abilities bloom!

IMPACT: You're delaying items getting thrown into the dump. More importantly, you're slowing the demand for new ones to be made in factories and shipped via diesel power.

BONUS TIP: Hoarding is sustainable! Designate a drawer, a box or a closet where you keep odds and ends for which you can't think of a purpose right now. It's incredible how often they prove to be perfect containers, tools, hairbands, display aids, pandemic masks or fancy-dress elements down the line.

A Final Few (Big) Ones

Lose the Car

Why is it that the people who complain most about how expensive their lives are always have cars?

I don't know who might be powerful enough to get the message across — a Pope? An Ayatollah? A President? A Chancellor? — but it's high time somebody told the world that owning your own vehicle is *not* non-negotiable. That we did without them for *thousands of years* until a tiny little slice of recent history. The sentence 'But I *need* my car' is, in a word, false.

We've gotten spoilt, that's all.

You know how and why private vehicles fit into this book, of course, but for the sake of completeness, let me quickly state the obvious. The machines themselves, the fuel that powers them and the supply chains for both are dirty. And having your own car costs you more unnecessary cash than anything I've mentioned apart from kids.

As governments try to control traffic and emissions, the fixed costs associated with driving are only going to go up. In most countries, these include compulsory insurance. And if you read my section on *that* topic, you know that's just one more good reason to climb out of the driver's seat.

Driving your own car is a lot like smoking: it's expensive and addictive. The best policy is never to start. The next-best policy is to kick the habit at as young an age as possible. Before the damage adds up.

How do we do that when it appears to be so hard? We're happy to buy the idea that fewer people should have cars. We agree (usually in the form of muttered swearing behind the wheel) that traffic needs to be brought under control. Yet we always think it's up to *other* people to make these things a reality! When it comes to the idea that it should be *us* making the change, we baulk. We say, 'I *would* give up the car, but…'

So hold it right there. The challenge is to break down this 'but' into its constituent parts, and then deal with each one of them. The 'buts' are almost always the result of us building a life around the idea of car ownership as a given. Perhaps we took a job in a part of town we can't reach by bus. Or we moved to the country for a quiet life, and the shops are no longer a short stroll away. As soon as we did that, we justified the idea that we 'needed' the car.

So now we need to reverse-engineer. Could it be that we should look for a job closer to home? Could we, on reflection, ride a horse or hitch a lift to the shops in the next town? Or start looking for retailers that deliver?

Am I going a step too far with this? Not if you take the title of this book to heart. And at the risk of repeating myself, it's mindless to dismiss big lifestyle changes because they sound like undiluted 'sacrifice'. Think about the Dalkey's Law equation. Might cutting out the car and taking that lower-paying job closer to home actually leave you with more money at the end of the month? Or could reducing to part-time (or convincing your boss to let you work more days from home) and taking an Uber to work three days a week put you in credit? When we take car ownership as a *constant* in the equation, we don't think about these things.

Another easy 'but' we use to justify vehicle ownership is the one that says we use the car to serve others. It's not *us* that needs the car! It's our kid's soccer team, whose players we volunteer to drive to matches. Or it's our disabled relative whom we take to appointments. These get-out clauses sit very well with our consciences. They allow us to use the car for ourselves 90% of the time and still think we're saints.

Regrettably, very few of us are in any danger of canonisation. In all but the rarest of cases, you're using altruism as a convenient end to justify the means. I know you're sincere. And I'm totally for helping out those who need support. But is it *really* only possible to render these services with a private vehicle? Couldn't you just as easily rent a car from SHARE NOW or similar? Could you rather help your relative achieve their tasks online, and then take them for a walk close to home?

When you tackle each one of the 'reasons' you 'need' a car, you'll very likely find there's an alternative that doesn't require you to have your own wheels. Even if you live in a country like South Africa, where people don't feel safe on public transport and sharing schemes have their challenges, there will be *some* other way. A different approach; some deal you can tweak. Worst-case scenario, the likes of Uber and (in Asia) Gojek are nearly everywhere.

There's another trap to watch out for in years to come: electric vehicles. These are already being pushed heavily by any number of stakeholders (including car manufacturers trying to keep your business) as the green alternative that will make you an ecological saint after all. Now, even without wading into the debate about whether 'electric fuel' is *really* cleaner than fossil fuels, it doesn't take long to see that replacing your carbon-burning engine with a battery is a cop-out. You're still enabling all manner of Earth-pillage for the rest of the car's materials, as well associated as factory and logistics emissions. And did you know how much microplastic lives in synthetic car tyres? You'll still be supporting all the damage that does. Need I go on? The idea that adding another private car to future scrapyards is somehow forward-thinking and planet-friendly just because it has a different power source is a marketing ruse. Don't fall for it. It's not as though electric cars are a solution for committed savers either: they *might* be cheaper to run, but I can still promise you that they'll cost you tens of thousands more than having no car at all.

Nobody ever said giving up the private car was an easy win. But it's a *huge* one — just look at the maths below. Even *without* factoring in fuel and the cost of the machine itself, you're looking at a sum of money substantial enough to invest in your future — be that a house, financial assets or your own company. Isn't that better than sitting in traffic, angrily, getting fat?

The best time to lose the car is *now*. Not next week. Not next year. That's about as likely to work for you as it will for someone trying to get off nicotine. So make your move on this even before you flip to the next section. If you need me to come and put sugar in your petrol tank, I'm up for it!

And to loop back to the discussion on sharing, couldn't you *at the very least* own a car in a pool with a neighbour or three? Or hire out your car through a platform like Turo? In exchange for planning your life a little and not always being able to grab the keys and go any time — there will always be on-demand services like taxis for moments of spontaneity! — you get to save half or a third of the monstrous sum below.

#1 TAKEAWAY Sell the car. Today. Now.

- Monthly fixed car costs (insurance, maintenance, parking, licensing, tax, depreciation): €120
- Available annual saving: €1440
- Bank credit by 40: **€27,360**

IMPACT: You're actively working against traffic, noise pollution, toxic emissions, oil spills...do I need to go on? Even when you rent out the car via a platform, you're doing good by giving other people options beyond automatically buying their own.

BONUS TIP: Bikes are not just for kids. (See also 'The Gym'.) True, they're not good for carrying groceries — but you can use a fraction of the thousands you've saved on the car to cover delivery fees.

BONUS TIP: Are you one of the large majority driving around solo nearly all of the time? If you insist on motorised transport, consider a scooter as a cheaper, more efficient compromise.

Wear a Jumper

This ought to be another short, sweet statement of something you already know, but which perhaps someone needs to say out loud.

(That someone will be me.)

Your energy bill is a major monthly or quarterly outgoing. There are a million cost permutations that will vary according to your country, city, local climate, the kind of energy that powers your home, how your provider bills and technical specifics such as your heating installations. I can't go into all of that here: there are plenty of books dedicated to the subject. What I will say is that I've yet to come across a situation where using less energy doesn't ultimately cut the big number at the bottom of your statement.

And even if it didn't, there remains the fact that the simplest, least controversial way for us to address the problem of dirty energy is to use less of the stuff. If we put half as much effort into this as we do arguing about whether solar beats nuclear, half our troubles would vanish regardless of who's right.

So that's two good reasons — both of them on the cover of this book — why wearing more layers is better than cranking up the heating. Either one of them is good enough on its own if you ask me.

I'm not saying you should freeze all the way through the peak of winter, but a smarter clothes policy could let you get away with a month or two less heating in spring and autumn. And an all-round lower heat setting.

(If you're in a hot country, your air conditioning and fans take a similar toll. Are you in a position to walk around the house in your underwear? Could you dive into the pool or sea every so often? Change your routine so you take a siesta during the hottest hours? All of the above?)

If heating water is costing you cash, you could (whisper it) shower every second or third day instead of daily. In winter, it's unlikely that you've sweated yourself into a stink. In summer, a fresh-water swim will often do the job. The idea of a daily wash, remember, is only a very recent one!

Like so much of this book, changes like this are simply down to breaking out of habit or developing a slightly adjusted mindset. They're *really* easy.

Other energy savings can be quick, one-off wins. Checking your fridge temperature and making sure it's full as can be. (A reserve stock of beers is always good for unexpected visitors.) See if there are any water-boiler settings you can adjust — perhaps you're heating more water than you'll ever use?

Then there are the bigger opportunities to make fundamental change. Maybe you live in a place where solar energy is viable. Look into the evolving options with regard to smart meters. I could go on — but I'd rather leave the technical stuff to the specialists. I just want to remind you that exploring the options could be well worth the time: Dalkey's Law and all that.

Finally, remember that living alone is an indulgence when it comes to bills. Adding another person isn't going to double your costs. Especially with regard to heating, where an extra body or four in the house hardly makes any difference — apart from having someone to split the bill with. I don't believe bill-sharing is a reason *per se* to move into a cottage with five rowdy students (or indeed a partner), but if you *are* in a phase of life where you're weighing up your living arrangements, it's one argument in favour of cohabitation.

#1 TAKEAWAY We're all more or less aware of how to cut our energy consumption. The big step is to start taking the task seriously.

- Monthly cost of your heating: €50
- Available annual saving if you achieve a 20% reduction: €120
- Bank credit by 40: **€2280**

IMPACT: The less energy you use, the fewer fossil fuels might get burned at some power station. Or maybe you could help shrink operations at your local nuclear facility!

BONUS TIP: Leave the oven door wide open after you've cooked something in winter. It's heat you've already paid for, so use it to warm the room!

Travel Smarter

Saving money when you travel needs a book all by itself – which is why I wrote one! You'll find details about *Monte Carlo for Vagabonds* at the end of this volume. That's where I share my (often quite extreme) experiences and philosophy in this area at far greater length. So I won't be going into very much detail here.

When you think about the trips you take, though, consider how so many of the themes I've touched on in this volume crop up in compressed form. You will have short-term decisions to make about whether to use a car, whether to take insurance and what food to buy. You'll be eating in restaurants more often than usual, and dealing with all that this entails. You'll have opportunities to do free stuff — or not. The friends or partners with whom you travel can have a greater-than-usual effect on your outgoings. And yes, taxi situations may arise.

Most of the spending and saving opportunities when we travel are just special variants of the everyday ones we've already looked at. It's pretty easy to see how and where they apply on holiday. Just like it does at home, making your own sandwich on your vacation in France will save you money compared to the supermarket version. You already know my opinion on upgrading the car rental insurance. Find out when free museum night is. And so on.

Just to be clear, I'm not at all against the 'Go on, we're on holiday!' mentality. This is a great time to treat yourself. But, as I always say, the more you save on boring stuff, like printing out maps and booking details so you can go without GPS upgrades and mobile roaming, the more you've got for extra ice creams! If you decide that your holiday is the reason you've been saving so purposefully for the rest of the year, then that's great. (It's at least as justifiable as driving racing cars!) Just make sure it's a conscious decision, and that you're absolutely happy with the consequences.

One biggie worth mentioning is, obviously, the distance you travel. Flying to the other side of the world is typically far more costly in both financial and environmental terms. Given this, I don't think it should be more than a five-yearly treat for anyone. We don't even enjoy it! Flying is a really, *really* costly way to be grumpy and cramped for hours on end, polluting the air as you go.

Nearly all of us were forced by COVID-19 to cut out long-distance travel. The question is, did you see that as a temporary torture or as an opportunity to question how much you *really* missed the pleasures of airports and planes? For me, travel restrictions were a blessing in disguise: I learned that the country in which I live has enough amazing destinations and experiences to keep me going for years. I learned just how many places you could reach by rail, bus or bike. I feel no inclination to rush back into the pre-pandemic habits which — let's not forget — allowed the virus to spread across the world the way it did. If we weren't so fond of flying, it could never have travelled so far, so fast. I like to think there's a lesson in that.

Happily, there's a growing trend (at least in enlightened societies) to holiday closer to home. You should look into it if you haven't already. Are there options you can reach by train or other shared transport? It might sound lame, but that's only because one generation of humanity got really spoilt for a few years.

One example: cycling holidays are a cheap, healthy way to see a region whilst barely moving the emissions dial. Don't dismiss them as only for the super-fit: some routes are flatter than you think — and who says you need to do 100km a day anyway? Nor is sharing the road with scary cars and trucks always necessary. If you live in Europe, for example, why not check out which of the epic EuroVelo routes passes near your home?

As for accommodation, do you *really* need the city centre Airbnb that has all the nice touches? You're only going to sleep and shower there, right? Are the kids going to appreciate those decorative vases — or break them? If a cheaper room's 'suburban location' means taking the bus into town, so what? That's a quick-win Dalkey's Law Gig. And you might well be getting a more realistic taste of local life into the bargain.

Here the purpose of your vacation and choice of travel companion will have an influence – I'd advise against a youth hostel dorm for your honeymoon! But in general, it's a good idea to know your priorities and set yourself a personal limit, just like in restaurants. The marvellous flip side to this apparent austerity? A series of small savings can add up to enough to pay for several more holidays!

#1 TAKEAWAY Define a threshold of what you're willing to spend per night for accommodation on trips. (Mine is €40.) Avoid temptation simply by applying this to your search filters when hunting on Airbnb or similar.

- Saving per week-long trip if you drop Airbnb 'per night' threshold by €10: €70
- Available annual saving if you take three trips: €210
- Bank credit by 40: **€3990**

IMPACT: Take your pick! If you've been naughty and flown to your holiday, perhaps think about ways you can offset that when you've reached your destination.

BONUS TIP: Don't give away money on card fees and ATM fees when travelling abroad! Apart from old chestnuts like not withdrawing cash with a credit card, explore newer options like Revolut. These are quietly killing cheeky bank charges, for example with mobile payment accounts that let you shift your money between currencies at negligible cost. You might soon find you don't need the local cash at all!

BONUS TIP: If you're set on going abroad, then pick a country with a weak currency or low prices.

BONUS TIP: If you go over your personal accommodation limit, just cancel it out by going under it the next night! As with just about everything in this book, it's the average that counts.

BONUS TIP: An apartment with a kitchen beats a hotel room almost every time! With zero cooking facilities, a hotel room basically forces you to eat every meal in a restaurant. Even if the apartment costs a little more (though usually it won't), consider the savings you can make by being able to make your own sandwich, salad or simple pasta at lunchtime.

Find a Savings Account

Since you're now going to have a lot more cash in your bank account at the end of every month, it's a good idea to think about where you're going to keep it!

You might decide to invest a lot of that extra money in some way or another, and that's grand. But don't get stuck up Asset Creek without a coin! Investments (including pensions) can fluctuate to the point that they might even disappear overnight. The happenings of 2020 were an uncomfortable reminder of that. So don't diss cash.

If you're going to keep some proper money in the bank, then you may as well choose an account that will give you some reward. Attractive interest rates have been pretty hard to find in recent years, but they're still available in some countries. So check your local market. See what's on offer.

Remember that accounts which restrict access to your money in exchange for decent interest, which perhaps you dismissed as dangerous before, may now be an option for you. Having switched on good savings habits, you should expect not to be counting the hours until payday! You should be finding lumps of cash in unexpected places. You can look forward to even your day-to-day account showing a satisfying tendency to swell without you even noticing. All of which means that if some portion of your wealth is on, say, 32-day notice, you know you're not going to starve while you wait for it.

I don't pretend to understand compound interest calculations. I failed that section of my maths exam at school, so I'll decline to offer you any sums at the end of this section. I'll just limit myself to saying that any interest you get is money for nothing more than the admin of opening the account and, if necessary, doing annual renewals of your deal. Which makes it a Dalkey's Law Gig worth checking out — and it *could* be worth more in the long term than is at first apparent.

#1 TAKEAWAY Shop around for the most favourable account(s) in which to grow your savings even further. Remember that instant access is no longer essential for you.

IMPACT: Not a lot, for once!

BONUS TIP: If you live in a country where Zimbabwe-style hyperinflation is a realistic possibility, that's not a reason to abandon cash. But it can definitely be a reason to try and save as much of it as possible in a foreign currency account! Again, check out some of the newer services making this easier than before. One example is Wise.

Conclusion

Last Word

You've now reached the end of this brief introduction to the art of saving. I truly hope it will be the turning point in your financial life — and see you living more responsibly into the bargain.

I'd be surprised if you're not wondering what the example figures at the end of the sections add up to. No need to run for the calculator: I wanted to answer that question too!

If we really assume that two people start out at 21, with one of them applying all of the changes in the examples until they're 40, and the other ploughing on as before, then the difference in their bank accounts as they enter their forties will be... **€256,731.50!**

There's a lot you can do with that kind of money, I'd say.

Of course, this is just a thought experiment. As I said upfront, the calculations were a bunch of illustrative examples. So the total, of course, is nothing other than a great big illustrative example! I realise that plenty of 21-year-olds don't have cars and don't plan on having kids (in which case they should be congratulated for being on a smart savings path already!). I know that real-life finances work differently. For one thing, if you were saving what works out to **€13,512** per year, you'd be well within your rights to spend plenty of it along the way. (I know I did! That's precisely the beauty of knowing you have habits in place that will regenerate your spend ultra-quick.)

But it's only by indulging in a slightly silly hypothesis like that — albeit, crucially, using perfectly realistic numbers — that you can really get a grasp of the impact (financial, this time!) saving can have. Because a process as fundamentally passive and negative as *not spending* a certain amount of money isn't going to make its effects apparent right away. The benefits of not having the latte sure aren't as tangible or tasty in the here and now as drinking that coffee. Which is *exactly* why people struggle to save.

So I hope these figures help paint a picture of what's going on in the background when you make strong savings choices. Use them as motivation. I hope they'll encourage you to make your own calculations to suit your own targets, if you feel inclined. Or just do as I did, and apply good savings principles safe in the knowledge that your bank account just seems to keep on climbing.

I never did a calculation. Nor did I have to be really smart. I just had to be willing to think my own thoughts, rather than follow those of the herd. I just had to hear the voices of logic and mathematics, rather than let them be drowned out by the louder noises our lives press upon us. To spot the abundance of Dalkey's Law Gigs around me and understand how those small earnings added up. These habits, on their own, are enough for you to make significant progress.

How far can you go? If the numbers above look nuts, take a moment to multiply your annual salary or earnings by 19 years as well. We're so caught up in our monthly or annual income that practically nobody takes a moment to do that calculation.

Do this maths, and you're likely to discover that the amount you *earn* in this time is at least as surprising as the savings figure up above. It will redefine what's possible.

Once you've set yourself up to save substantial amounts, you are of course well on the way to being able to do far more exciting things than squirrel money away! Whether you want to retire young, work less, trade stocks, start a business, own a house, buy a Mercedes-Benz or simply have the financial freedom to do volunteering or meaningful work, it all starts with a basic ability to pile up some funds — even from a low base and given an unspectacular job. From there, safe in the knowledge that you can try things and it won't be the end of the world if you fail, you've got every chance of hitting real wealth. I look forward to hearing how you go — good results would be superb material for your review of this book!

But I do encourage you to stay humble, even if you succeed in your goals. There's at least one kind of saving we should never stop, no matter how financially secure we feel. Because we're more fragile and vulnerable than we like to believe. And we need to take better care of this planet we call home: neither pathogens nor pollution care whether you're rich or poor. Cash won't do you much good if you can't breathe the air. So don't *actually* buy a Mercedes-Benz, because that's a car, and, you know…

The End

Three Jolly Nice Ideas

Want to know what a lifetime of extreme budget travel is like? R.A. Dalkey shares his tips and adventures on the road in **Monte Carlo for Vagabonds**. Get the ebook, paperback or audiobook via books2read.com/montecarlo.

If you'd like to be informed when R.A. Dalkey publishes his next book, please join his mailing list at http://eepurl.com/ghcLDv.

Interested in an individual coaching session that will make you a better saver? Contact the author directly on rasher05@gmail.com.

About the Author

R.A. Dalkey *(nom de plume)* was born in Cape Town, holds British citizenship and now lives halfway up a steep, wooded incline on the edge of Vienna. Between growing up amidst the euphoria and disappointments of post-Apartheid South Africa and settling (Brexit-permitting...) in Austria at 35, he's lived in the USA, Australia and the UK.

An incorrigible dreamer, he's driven outback trucks in Australia, spent two years trying to be a professional golfer and slept rough everywhere from Monte Carlo to Siberia, visiting over 70 countries along the way. Including Ireland, where he cracked up every time he rode the DART train past a town called Dalkey, and an author name was born.

As for the occasional bout of work, he's known to do his fair share of editing magazines and writing. Under his own name, his words have been published by *GQ*, *Reader's Digest*, *The Sunday Times*, *Australian International Traveller*, *Die Presse*, *Autosport*, *Sports Illustrated* and Reuters, to name just a handful.

Also by R.A. Dalkey

Monte Carlo For Vagabonds (books2read.com/montecarlo)

Never Drive A Hatchback To Austria (books2read.com/austria)

The Road to Innamincka (books2read.com/trucking)

Acknowledgments

Now's the moment for me to give a hearty back-slap to those on my team! To every friend who has taken the time to give me feedback (especially the tricky 'that's crap' line) on text, cover designs, blurbs and more besides. Or even to lend a helping hand. I'm very highly obliged.

Particular mention must go to Catbot Design for their help in pulling the cover together in double-quick time during the COVID-19 lockdown. Thanks also to Suzanne Arnold for proofreading and editorial input.

And finally, in advance, to every reader who reviews and/or recommends my work. Even if you only send that link to one friend (your entire book club would also be fine...), it could make way more difference than you think.